IN THE NICK OF TIME

Sincerely

Nick Berryman

Tangmere /04.

First edition, published in 2000 by

WOODFIELD PUBLISHING
Woodfield House, Babsham Lane, Bognor Regis
West Sussex PO21 5EL, England.

ISBN 1-903953-12-X

9 781903 953129

In the
Nick of
Time

NICK BERRYMAN

Woodfield Publishing
BOGNOR REGIS · WEST SUSSEX · ENGLAND

I dedicate this book to my wartime colleagues who often imperilled their own lives endeavouring to save others.

Contents

ACKNOWLEDGEMENTS

I would like to thank all friends and family who have helped, supported and encouraged me during the production of this work. My special thanks go to:

My brother Alan, whose cartoons are published in this book.

Stephen Dunster, who was able to read the feelings of we aircrew survivors well enough to compose the poem *An Extraordinary Time and Place.*

My friend Trevor Lay, whose painting has been used as the front cover illustration. It captures to perfection that wonderful moment when the searcher finds the lost.

THE EARLY YEARS

To use a hackneyed phrase, I was born at a very early age and have progressed more by good luck than judgement ever since. From the word go, I was obviously destined to be a good Christian and honoured my father and mother.

My trouble was that, in my own estimation, I honoured them by just arriving. I loved them dearly and respected them for what they were: father as an up-and-coming London and Southwestern bank cashier at Walham Green, London, and mother because she was a good provider and beautiful to boot. The combination does not come too often and it took me 25 years to find out that I was a privileged child of my time – or any time for that matter.

Father had emerged from the Great War virtually unscathed. He had served his country well, joining Kitchener's "Your Country Needs You" army in 1915 and doing service in the Honourable Artillery Company. He spoke little about his war years, but in my teens I often showed interest and heard some tales of the horrors he witnessed with so many others: shelling, gas, mutilation and death, much of which I was to experience for myself at a later date, to father's deep regret. In those days, I am quite sure that in his mind he had fought a 'war to end all wars'. With the ending of hostilities in 1918, back he came to marry his beloved "Connie" and to start work again in the London and Southwestern Bank (later to be engulfed with other smaller banks into Barclay's).

Born in Wales during 1893, he was obviously a bit brighter than most at school in Mathematics. I discovered later however, and I wasn't bright, that he was pretty abysmal at everything else. His knowledge of History and Geography were, for a start, terrible. He would do my Maths homework (and only he could do it) in five minutes flat. Explaining patiently to me as he went, he also provided the occasional cuff round the ear and an outburst to my mother that his eldest son was a moron. When it came to advising me as to the geographical location of Kalgoorlie and its importance to the world, he was quite capable of telling me with much conviction and aplomb that it was in South Africa and that the South Wales Border Regiment had made a successful stand against the Hottentots there in 1901. My mother fortunately always seemed to be hovering around with several dictionaries, reference books and *Pear's Encyclopedia* to correct the information. Once correctly on paper my father became quite convinced that it was what he had said in the first place and if only I would "damn well listen instead of trying to read the football scores upside down on the back page of the *London Evening News* we shouldn't have had the misunderstanding anyway!"

However, there it was, not every boy's father could add six columns of pounds, shillings and pence and put the answer down while his son was still adding the pence! I suppose he had to be a bit larger than life. I had yet to get to know his sisters.

Born Reginald Wyndham, my father was the eldest son to William Lewis and Emily Kate Berryman, my grandparents. He was later followed by sister 'Butty', brother Cyril, sister 'Daisy', brother 'Willy', and sister 'Topsy'.

I remember little of my Grandfather, but he was a man of medium-to-short build and, at the age of sixty, showed physical signs of always having been well fed and watered; although watered is probably the wrong word, unless he drank a lot of it together with something he obviously preferred. He was known to enjoy his whisky, a habit which my grandmother obviously abhorred, being teetotal and a devout churchgoer. Grandfather's ample stomach always supported a waistcoat adorned with a large gold watch-chain. He, I think, was dogged by a bit of bad luck, or it could have been judgement, in his business life. Described on my father's Birth Certificate as a 'Draper', he ended his days selling Axminster carpet. Quite a good business I suppose, as most homes at the time were furnished with yards of cold shiny lino, and grandma, who always had the best and was somewhat indulged by the whole family, would not have liked too much lino.

Earlier in his days, grandpa had been in business for himself and at one time had seven ponies and traps for travelling sales in Merthyr and the surrounding villages which, in the 1900s, were deeply rooted in coal mining. From what has been said, his parting from this occupation was due to his over-trusting nature, the main problem having been a relative of his believed to have been a cousin. However, all was not lost, and before long he appears as the owner of a shop in Merthyr High Street (a photograph of which is still in existence) and another in the outlying 'Cefn' district of Merthyr. The building was at 193 High Street, Cefn Vaynor, Brecon, and was still there in 1989.

Born William Lewis Berryman in the year 1865 he was the grandson of Mark Berryman, a Cornishman from Towednack, who migrated to South Wales in search of work around 1815. Mark became a shopkeeper and carrier in Brecon. One of his sons – William's father, Matthew – was an iron miner and limestone quarryman, who was killed in a rock fall in Vaynor Quarry in 1896.

Apart from Grandfather, there were four other sons and four daughters from the marriage: Evan, Minnie, Leah, Arthur-Matthew, Mark, Rebecca, Mary and Edward.

Grandfather William stayed in Wales to earn his living whilst Mark emigrated to Perth, Australia, and Arthur-Matthew went off to Canada. Both Mark and Matthew obviously did very well, as 'Uncle' Matthew occasionally returned to the UK in the 1930s to see his kinsfolk and distribute largesse all round. He certainly stood my father a few much appreciated good lunches. Australian Mark was seldom mentioned, but he evidently did not waste a lot of time as his son and grandson are now the proprietors of one of Perth's most prestigious motor agents dealing mostly in Mercedes.

Knowing the family's capabilities in that direction, I suspect that Mark began 'horse dealing' in about 1885 and progressed to the motor car, as the business has been long established.

In passing, the clock has now turned full circle, as a great-great-granddaughter from part of the 'Australian' family was educated at St Swithun's School, Winchester, alongside my granddaughter, Victoria – it's a small world!

Back to Grandfather William resident in Wales, he successfully courted and finally married into the Hand family. The Hands came from Wiltshire, and certainly my Grandmother Emily was born in that county. Great-grandfather Hand, however, was a policeman, later to become Deputy Chief Constable of Breconshire finally retiring in 1918. His marriage to a diminutive Welsh woman, often clad in traditional Welsh costume, produced Emily and others in her union with great-grandfather. The scene and saga are now set.

MY FATHER

At this point in the story, Grandparents William and Emily are resident in Merthyr and following their chosen business occupation, whilst during their leisure moments producing seven children, one of whom died in infancy. The others, already mentioned, were to live in the family home of 10 Norman Terrace, Merthyr Tydfil.

Reginald Wyndham, my father, went to school in nearby Cyfartha, which now houses a large museum. At the age of 17, he then went off to an unknown uncle on his mother's side, to try his hand at being a "farmer's boy". A more unlikely candidate for such an occupation would have been hard to find. After a month, he made swiftly off to London and landed a job with The London and Southwestern Bank in the year of 1912.

Victorian-parented fathers probably found it imprudent to pass on too much information regarding their teenage and early adulthood, and the years 1910 to 1915 in my father's life are a complete mystery to me. From treasured family photographs however, and knowledge of the man's character, I can at least conjecture.

Handsome he certainly was, and with his naughty sense of humour I can only think that the ladies of Walham Green could have been set off into something of a dither. Though not a natural sportsman, he played the socially acceptable game of tennis at a

Grandmother Emily, as portrayed by my brother Alan.

reasonable standard, belonged to clubs and did all the things that such clubs encompass.

Summer, I think, must have been his favourite time for sport. He loved the River Thames and was wont to go off punting on many occasions, always dressed for the part. Picnics on a river were one of his favourite pastimes. Dirty winter games like soccer or hockey were out, and he couldn't "punt a soccer ball for nuts!"

He obviously had his own idea about winter sports, but he liked the theatre and theatre came under that heading. He was no snob, but although he enjoyed "doing things properly" he was just as much at home in Music Halls as he was at the traditional theatre, and again he dressed for the occasion. I still have his silk white scarf, white cotton gloves and opera hat which, with built in collapsible spring top, has been a source of great amusement to successive generations of children.

Not adverse to a pint or a short (whichever he could afford) it was not unknown for him to cross swords with the Law. One Boat Race Night, the Oxford Crew and the Vine Street Police Station figured in one of his off the cuff chats. I suspect he may have later regretted it, as he had no wish to encourage by example an elder son who was, by nature, only too capable of following suit (and who did so some 20 years later). In both our cases, however, we got off with a caution, a form of police disciplinary action which sadly appears to have disappeared along with the cuff around the back of the head.

It must have been about this time that father met my mother, a strictly brought up young lady of some 20 years of age from a rather poorer family than his own, living in Fulham. As one of seven children, mother had got this far by learning to survive. Unlike my father's family, there was never any money to spare. Dedication to cleanliness and education were bywords in the Rogers family. Clothes were either passed down or made, and the slightest refusal to eat up one's food at table resulted in six other forks descending upon the plate in question. I never knew Grandfather George Rogers but he described himself on my mother's Birth Certificate as a 'Journeyman' (Hot Water Fitter).

In 1893 he was resident in New Road, Marylebone, and was regularly employed by the 'Upper Crust' society of Central and West London including Eaton Square. His wife Minnie (nee McGowran) had already presented him with a son Leslie and a daughter Winnie when my mother arrived on the scene. She was then followed, fairly quickly, by Stanley and Bertie, but it wasn't until some 12-14 years later that Ernie and Bobbie were born.

It would appear that Grandfather and Minnie, whom I knew well and loved dearly, had a somewhat stormy marriage, but typical of the Rogers family, the children were too busy getting on with their own lives to care too much.

Grandfather Rogers' work often took him away from London. I think this was because the Eaton Square set sometimes needed him to work in their country homes. He was well respected for his high quality of work.

When he was away on these trips, it appears that, out of loneliness for her beloved spouse, Minnie would take to the bottle (not excessively, but she enjoyed it). Then, upon his return, having discovered things had not gone as he would have wished, there would be ructions. It was not long before he found an excuse to be off again.

The children do not appear to have suffered from all this. As I grew up I knew all my uncles and aunts very well, in fact much better than those on the Berryman side. Every one of them was strongly self-disciplined, self-reliant and capable. A bit on the hard side perhaps, but certainly humorous and loving.

The family home was, by then, 19 Betteridge Road, Fulham. My father swore that he could run the whole length of the road in 15 seconds flat when grandfather's boot was behind him. Timing was never his forte, and daughters in those days had to be home by 10:00 pm.

Grandfather Rogers finally left Minnie and died alone in the City of Chester during 1930. He evidently had style, I gather he was known locally as 'The Gentleman'. A loner I think, and I'm sorry I never knew him. Grandmother Minnie pressed on as far as her limited means would allow. Although poor and often comforted by a bottle, she always loved me, her grandson, and was proud of my boyhood achievements. She was fun and, as a newly-commissioned Pilot Officer in 1942, I sadly saluted as she was lowered into her grave.

The dawning of 1915 signalled the start of a new era. A poignant year for many and no less so for my father Reginald Wyndham. He left behind him the Bank, tennis, river and theatre, as he departed for France to defend King and Country. He was a good communicator, lover and loving father. My family have over 100 war postcards, posted between 1915 and 1919 giving his whereabouts in war-torn France.

Leave was non-existent. Constantly in the front-line trenches, he never suffered the traumas of having to bayonet a Hun, but there was no doubt that short rations, mud, shell holes, dead bodies, lice and filth were the order of the day. The horrors of the war made a great impact on him. Certainly, my brother and I were never allowed to waste food on any account, even to the extent of near fanaticism. He said he had seen men fight for a crust of bread. It must have been terrible for him to be dirty. He hated it, and the fact he was not circumcised was a constant source of annoyance to him. "Had to spit on the damn thing to keep it clean", he would say, as he later exhorted me to greater personal hygiene.

It has always amazed me that he never rose in rank or became commissioned. Certainly, World War II forces would have required him in commissioned rank, but then that was a different War.

When Reginald eventually returned to England in 1919, having also served in the Army of Occupation, the London and South-western Bank welcomed him back with open arms as cashier in the Walham Green branch. He no doubt set the feminine hearts of Fulham fluttering once again.

Father joined the Infantry Division of the Honourable Artillery Company (HAC) as a Private Soldier in the First World War. He was trained at the Tower of London Headquarters, and then spent the rest of the War in or near the front line in France, ending finally with the Army of Occupation in Germany. The HAC is an old and distinguished Regiment, and at the time of the First World War it had been specially re-organised as an active-service Officers' Training Unit. This was in common with one or two other special regiments then, such as the Inns of Court Regiment and the Artists Rifles, which also recruited in all ranks from the professions.

Like many others in his position, Reg probably had no great ambition to be commissioned. He was in good company, and with the Bank making up his Army pay to his full civilian income, he may well have thought himself as altogether better off than the officers standing in the mud beside him. Whatever he thought, he remained in the ranks throughout the War, and was not to be commissioned until joining the Home Guard in the Second World War.

One day at the front, a French unit passed through the HAC trenches. Unlike the HAC, they had been fed. One of the French soldiers dropped a piece of bread in the mud as he passed by. Reg promptly rescued it from beneath the marching feet. With most of the mud scraped off, it was the best hunk of bread he had ever tasted. Later the HAC was taken out of the front line for rest and re-equipment. Still desperately hungry, Reg tried the Toc H, the Church Army, and every canteen he could find. He was turned away by them all except the Salvation Army. In later life he never failed to contribute to their cause. When they were collecting, he always bought their "War Cry" magazine, and he gave his children hell if a single scrap of food was ever left on their plates.

On another occasion the HAC was ordered to provide an armed guard for visiting Royalty. Being well behind the line at the time, the party happened to include a number of ladies with their ladies-in-waiting. Reg recalls a friend of his standing guard outside one of the bedrooms on the first evening.

He said, "The ladies murmured 'goodnight sentry', as they retired and shortly after I heard that most heavenly of feminine sounds, not heard for a very long time."

"What was that?" asked Reg, possibly misjudging the answer. "Why? A Maiden saying her prayers."

Eventually the 'gentlemen rankers' experiment in World War I was considered a failure. With so many potential leaders packed together in the firing line, there was an appalling and concentrated loss of life. Reg was gassed, often half-starved, and was indeed fortunate to have survived.

Today the Gunner Division of the Honourable Artillery Company still exists as a corps d'elite on a 'Territorial' basis, maintaining its old traditions, and frequently prominent on State occasions (eg firing the gun salutes at the Tower of London). They still maintain the tradition of gentlemen-rankers, all ranks being on equal terms except when 'on parade,' but never again will they fight in this particular formation. The experiment was far too costly.

MY MOTHER

Connie Rogers, later to be my mother, had all this time been beavering away in Derry & Tom's as a cashier in the Counting House.

She combined modesty and considerable academic achievement with her undoubted beauty. A regular prize-winner at school and commended for good conduct and punctuality, she won first prize in the Essay Competition open to all London County Council Schools. First class also in arithmetic, she later developed into a most capable accountant and could easily have become qualified if she had not married young. This was in the days when the place of a wife was very definitely in the home, and Connie was nothing if not dutiful.

I do not think that Derry & Tom's exists today, but between the wars it was situated at the top of Kensington High Street which was just about opposite Church Street. I have no doubt that the imposing building is now under the auspices of another but more modern business name. The distance from 19 Betteridge Road must be all of 4 miles and I was regularly reminded that, in order to save the bus fare, mother walked at least one way each day; and six days constituted a week's work.

She was paid 2s 6d a week (twelve and a half pence in decimal coinage). Connie's legs obviously became very strong, as she was seldom to be off them for the rest of her days. She was industrious and could move pretty fast. Not fast enough, however, to escape the attentions of Reginald Wyndham who pursued her relentlessly for another 12 months. She took a fair bit of stick from her brothers, who to say the least were down to earth, and who had also returned from the war. To cap it all, they had been reared in a somewhat different environment from Reggie, not that the Rogers boys were not smart. They certainly were, but in a different, more casual way.

The exception was younger brother 'Ernie' who was probably one of the most immaculate men I have yet to meet. Even the underside of his shoes were polished. At this time, he was the second youngest and probably had not a great deal to say. Sisters Winnie and Bobbie enjoyed the experience of my parents' courtship and both adored Reg for the remainder of his days. He used to arrive to court Connie, attired in bank clerk's suiting and very debonair with hat and white gloves. For the time being however, sing-songs round the piano in the front room cemented the relationship to everyone's ultimate satisfaction. True to form, Reggie took Connie to the altar on 6th April 1920, thus not wasting even one day of a tax year for marriage allowance.

MY FAMILY

Waldegrave Road, Fulham, was Reggie's bachelor abode, but as a married couple they soon took up residence in a large block of flats still to be seen today. These were Waldemar Avenue Mansions, situated on the Hammersmith side of Putney Bridge about 300 yards East of Fulham Football Ground, and there I was born two years later on the 1st September 1922.

When describing my place of birth, I used always to say Putney, which for some indescribable reason I considered a bit up-market to Fulham. Today however, this is not the case as Fulham is the domain of theatre and TV personalities. Certainly 19 Betteridge Road, for which dear Grandma paid the equivalent of one pound twenty pence a week rent, was on the market in 1988 for two hundred and twenty three thousands pounds.

My father's bank manager at Walham Green was a delightful elderly bachelor by the name of Wilde. He lived at Corner House, Dryburgh Road, Putney and was attended by a housekeeper and a cook. The house has now been demolished, and a large block of very expensive flats and the Putney Swimming Pool cover the area. Mr Wilde, in his great wisdom, took an immediate liking to me, and in 1924 deposited a sum of money in an insurance policy, to mature when I was 18. At the same time he wrote me a letter. I quote:

My Dear Neville

I have taken up the enclosed National Savings Certificate in your name on your 2nd Birthday so that when you have grown up you may have an amount accumulated to help you on in life. By that time I may possibly have passed away but you will have life before you and I trust that what I have now done for you will help you on to an honourable and successful career. Always remember however that such success will depend mainly on yourself. Therefore persevere and learn all you can. Lead a straight and truthful life and cultivate a sense of duty towards God and Man.

This is the advice, with the best of good wishes, for your welfare.

Your affectionate Uncle

It typifies the man and the world in which I lived until adulthood. I consider it one of the nicest letters I have ever received, and the wisdom contained therein I have used to best advantage. I have no doubt that the reader could pick out one or two bits of advice which accidentally escaped my attention.

In 1925, my father was moved to the newly-constituted Barclays Bank at 311 North End Road, Fulham, at the corner of Lillie Road and we lived over the Bank premises. I was three and a half years of age and rapidly becoming a North End Road Adventurer. I awaited the arrival of mother's second child and I remember her being a bit plump, but the bulge turned out to be my brother.

The boy was an encumbrance from the word go. He was born at a very cold time of year, 2nd November 1926. This necessitated my removal from the huge warm fires in the cosy dining room of 311 North End Road to the care of Grandma Minnie (Nan) at 19 Betteridge Road where gas lights, small fires and candle-lit bedrooms prevailed. I loved Nan however, and the additional bonus was that my nice Aunt Bobbie was there as well. She was a good looking, dark haired lady approaching 19.

The digs were good and I had a great addiction to tinned pineapple, but at 6d a tin it was hard to come by at home. However, at No. 19 the tins seemed to grow on the bushes in the back garden together with white bread and butter. What more could a chap want for tea?

The upstairs bedrooms were obviously too cold or remote for such as me, and it was here in a ground-floor bedroom that I first experienced the warmth of feminine contact, other than my Mother of course. After kneeling beside the bed to say my prayers, I was put to bed early and the candle blown out, but sometime later another candle would arrive, and Aunt Bobbie would snuggle into the large double bed beside me. I soon fell asleep again, safe and reassured.

In order to wake well in time for work each morning, she entrusted the operation to the largest, noisiest, ticking alarm clock I have ever come across. Even now I can still hear that strident sharp tick and the shrill bell that woke us in the morning.

Bobbie was soon away. A dash down the garden path to the outside lavatory, wherein hung copious amounts of newspaper threaded by string. Splashing noises in the adjoining scullery, the hiss of a kettle, a quick kiss and she was gone. Nan and I used to walk in the public parks quite a lot and I was seldom warm. This went on for several days before I was returned to my family circle. Yes, a brother was going to be an encumbrance!

With the coming of my brother, henceforth to be known as Alan, the immediate family was formed as it would continue for the next 39 years.

OF MOTORCYCLES AND STEAM ENGINES

My mother's desire for her second child to be a daughter had not been granted and her disappointment was to show in her upbringing of Alan William for some three or four years, this fact being well recognised by her side of the family. Early photographs showed him always with a much longer hair style than was normal for a boy in 1926 and his dress was fine and decorative. Alan was endowed with a good head of hair like my father and the Berrymans, not fine and wispy as mine was; which had come straight from the Rogers' males. Perhaps with the exception of the youngest, Uncle Ernie, whose sister Bobbie was also well endowed with a fine head of dark hair.

My mother's desires for a daughter were further compounded by the arrival of our first housemaid, Jane Freeman from Hammersmith. Jane too would have preferred a girl to look after, if only to offset the four and a half years old other load of trouble she was to be partly responsible for. Their joint struggles, however, were to come to nought. At the age of three whilst on holiday at a farm near Bristol, Alan was soon driving the cows with raucous shouts and seemed constantly in need of a wash to remove the cow and pig dung, not to mention the odd chicken turd. Connie's small battle was over. She definitely had two boys.

Father meanwhile was struggling financially, with the transition from motorcycle & side car to motor car as his leisure pursuit and for family transport. Alan never experienced the three earlier motor cycle years. An AJS 350 with sidecar was my father's pride and joy. I can just remember days out and holidays in company with his brother Cyril from Wales and brother-in-law

Reflecting upon Cyril's manner of driving, that must have been where Ken learned to hang on to anything. I was later to see him ride most kinds of animal across the Welsh mountainside; goats, large sheep, shaggy ponies, fat cows, the odd bullock, you name it, he could ride it, (once again to my envy). As you see, I was being reared as a 'townee' more used to busy streets than peaceful countryside.

Ted (Winnie's husband) complete with families and similarly equipped with three wheels. It was with great envy I used to watch my cousin Ken, two years older than I, climb onto the pillion seat of his father's combination, whilst I was confined with my mother in a sidecar. Reflecting upon Cyril's manner of driving, that must have been where Ken learned to hang on to anything. I was later to see him ride most kinds of animal across the Welsh mountainside; goats, large sheep, shaggy ponies, fat cows, the odd bullock, you name it, he could ride it, (once again to my envy). As you see, I was being reared as a 'townee' more used to busy streets than peaceful countryside.

These days out were full of excitement, for the roads were not all that smooth and with three motorcycle combinations being ridden in convoy, one or other was always breaking down or getting a puncture. The South and Southwest of England and certainly all the Inns, were well explored. Evening, turning to night, after such an excursion was a particularly trying time. The excitement of the day was over, sand dunes had been leaped, trees climbed, rivers forded and the journey home seemed interminable – only an occasional glimmer of hope entered a tired body, a pull into a country pub where I was rewarded with a lemonade and an arrowroot biscuit. The latter cost 1d and was as large as a saucer. It appeared that such a visit was considered necessary by parental nocturnal adventurers. Nobody seemed to carry water, which added weight I suppose, and when the carbide headlamp went out there was always an expeditious manner of dampening the carbide powder which gave off gas and when lit, lighted our way home. My father always swore blind that the light was better after he had peed in the container. The light may have been good, but the odour could have been improved.

In 1927, about January, the first Bullnose Morris Cowley XX193 appeared. An elegant dark blue with brown leather seats, two doors, a canvas hood and a dickie seat. To mother's delight and relief, it also had electric lamps. About a month before, dad had owned a Calthorpe. It was not a great success and it ended its brief association with my father whilst transporting Grandmother Rogers. A wheel fell off in the New Kings Road, Fulham. Dad was not a man to be trifled with and it was dismissed with ignominy.

Barclays Bank now sent my father to the Millbank branch, not far from the Tate Gallery on the Thames Embankment, as Chief Cashier. He had to find a home quickly, and he purchased a little box of a house near Perivale Park, North Ealing. Nobody liked the home from the word go.

From there, I went to school for the first time and learned to ride a two-wheeled bike. I didn't like the school, dad didn't like the house and I don't think he was too keen on Millbank either. Mother was all right, she had Alan to see to. There was only one thing for dad to do – get a transfer. So get a transfer he did. He was promoted to 'Clerk in Charge' of Barclays Bank, 220 Horn Lane, Acton. He quickly sold the unloved house and we moved into Bank premises again.

Horn Lane, Acton, proved to be a boy's paradise. I could see immediately that the area was full of potential. Situated at the very top of Horn Lane at the junction with Emmanuel Avenue, a fair-sized branch, it had very large living accommodation covering three floors and a large high-walled rear yard. The main Great Western Railway, London to the West, was a stone's throw away with adjoining sidings for rail tracks and North Acton Station stood atop the bridge linking the road from Acton to Harlesdon. The almost constant thunder of the mighty steam express engines, shrieking whistles and clouds of white steam were a tremendous source of interest. I was now eight years old and could appreciate speed. If you were quick, great names like King George V, Caernavon Castle and Stirling Castle could be spotted, all in a morning, as they sped on their journeys. As we dangled our legs over the bridge, the smell of the smoke and steam became perfume itself and the hands and faces of myself and friend got blacker and blacker. The Walls Ice Cream factory was only one hundred yards away and the to-ing and fro-ing of the three-wheeled box trikes with their peaked-capped, white-coated riders was another source of amusement. With a loaded trike, some of the smaller salesmen couldn't pedal the weight over the bridge if going North, but they used to go like heck down the other side eager to get to their sales round and street area. It must have been a hard way to earn a living and I remember discussing with a friend that apart from the obvious advantage of carrying a constant supply of delicious and varied ice creams, the occupation was best avoided in later life.

SCHOOL DAYS AND HOLIDAYS

Schooling meant my going to Lancaster House and Alan to Shirley House (Miss Streddars), private schools both within walking distance of our home. Our maidservant Jane, had left and Mary from Dunstable had arrived. As she took Alan to school, I went off alone.

I had two particular friends, Geoff Smith and Maurice McVety. Maurice, the bootmaker's son, always had money. Geoff and I had not a 'sou', which explains why I used to pinch the odd sherbet dab from the little sweet-shop across the road. My father suspected that my pocket money was going rather a long way and took me back to the shop one day to enquire whether I had too much for the money I had been given. The dear, sweet old lady who owned the shop looked at my collection of spoils, and knowing quite well that I had at least twice as much as I should have had for 2d, assured my father that I only had the correct amount, no more or less. I never stole another thing from that day on.

Schooling took a back seat to other pursuits and Maurice, Geoff and I spent our days looking for mischief. We were regularly chased off the tracks in the railway sidings. Visits to the local Parks and the joy of all: an entertainment known as 'Getting a Whippy'.

Only half a mile away was the Western Avenue/main London Road to Oxford, the A40. To travel it today, as I sometimes do, is a hair-raising nose-to-tail traffic problem, but in 1930 traffic was few and far between. The Odeon Cinema at the bottom of the hill was the starting place for the operation. As large, heavily-laden lorries used to change gear to climb the long hill before them, our swift legs had us tearing up to and behind the tailboard of the vehicle and with shouts of triumph like howling Dervishes, we hauled ourselves aloft. The challenge was not to be seen by the driver or the police and I, personally, was never caught, but how I escaped death under those pounding wheels I shall never know. At the top of the hill, as the lorry gained speed, we leapt off and descended the hill for another 'Whippy'. No wonder Richmal Crompton wrote the 'William' books.

At Lancaster House School I had fallen in love with my teacher, Miss Hallowes, and had an obsession to find out what colour knickers she wore. Standing round her desk one day doing arithmetical tables with the rest of the class, I dropped my handkerchief. A quick bend down to retrieve, a glance upwards and at last I knew. They were pink, and long ones at that! Obviously, my lust was sated, for I cannot remember showing even the remotest interest in the female sex for the next five years (apart from kissing Diedre Smith under the shade of the front garden hedge, that is).

No, sport it was for me. In 1930 I won a cup for the 100 yards dash at Barclays Bank Sports Day and captained Lancaster House Under-Ten Soccer Team. I took up boxing, got a punch ball for Christmas and set fire to the plumber's hat with a jumping cracker. Well, this would have been sport if he hadn't been a customer at the Bank.

Summer pursuits included pounding a tennis ball against the back yard wall. If tennis was not in favour, football certainly was. I could blow 'em up and lace 'em up, and I could kick well with both feet. I was 30 years of age before I parted with an inflation adaptor (non-return valve) from my back trouser pocket and I still have it today. The lower rear windows of the Bank of course took some pounding. I was in constant trouble and often my pocket money was stopped. Sometimes when this happened, I was grateful to horse-drawn traffic. A couple of trips up Emmanuel Avenue with bucket and shovel soon redressed the situation, as horse manure sold at 2d a bucket. This did not appear to meet with my father's approval, as by this time he had been promoted to Manager. The youngest in the whole of Barclays Bank – not bad for a chap who never knew where Kalgoorlie was.

It was thought desirable that I should learn to play the piano, but all I learned in two years was 'The Bluebells of Scotland' and where middle C was on the keyboard (first note to the right of the lid lock). This venture also cost my suffering father a pair of spectacles, as my teacher assured him that I couldn't read the notes properly. My piano teacher was Alan's schoolma'am, Miss Streddar. Knowing Alan, how could she possibly envisage a shocking liar like me as his brother! I had to persevere with glasses as a penance but after a further year I managed to tread on them, at the same time assuring my father that I was cured anyway. I proved it by reading the bottom line of the Daily Express at five feet.

Sometime about this period, having proved that I was responsible enough to get to Lancaster House and back on my own, my father decided that his family should get to know me better and vice-versa. One sunny day, I was despatched in a Royal Blue coach to his native Wales. Another traveller was asked to keep an eye on me and, with my sandwiches, my great adventure began.

'Royal Blues' were the last word in luxury travel in those days and I obviously felt quite a boy. The day was warm and the surrounding roads and fields sped by my inquisitive eyes. The very thought of doing this on my own was idyllic enough, but the thought of opening my sandwiches whenever I wished was a thought to be savoured. We stopped at Oxford, Cheltenham and Gloucester, and each time I alighted, I walked round the coach with a proprietary air.

Upon arrival, I began to wish I had not walked round the coach so much. Aunt 'Butty' had arrived home from Nigeria where she was resident with her husband Gordon and took me over (determined that my arrival would not disturb the peaceful pattern of home life). For a whole week, I was hauled up one Brecon Beacon after another and was told that it was all very good for me, being a town bred boy with a pale face. I have never liked mountains or walking overmuch since.

The bonuses were morning tea in bed with two biscuits served by Eva the maidservant and the odd visit to Uncle Willie's home where I met cousins John and Pat. The teas were good; the milk came in huge jugs, whilst tinned salmon and very sweet tomatoes appeared on the menu twice, to my obvious delight.

One rainy day, I was allowed to practically strip the harmonium. It had not worked for years. I must have had some sort of mechanical brain even then, and to everyone's surprise it worked afterwards.

We attended church three times on Sunday. Granddad didn't talk to me a lot but Grandma used to give me a 'Joey' (silver 3d piece) to spend in Mrs Harris' sweet shop. Everyone was very kind but I was glad to return to smoky old London.

I was no great scholar, unlike Alan who was a studious boy and conducted himself with a certain amount of decorum. It was now about 1933. Whilst visiting the Odeon Cinema, Northfields, to see "Lives of a Bengal Lancer", Alan complained he was unable to read the sub-titles at the end of the film. I shall never forget my father soon afterwards in the car park after Alan had failed to read the film poster which had lettering two feet high, informing my mother that the boy was "... blind, I tell you. Blind"! Well, a visit to the optician did confirm he needed glasses and to this day still requires optical aid.

Schooling for me was causing my father concern. Hoping to improve my capabilities, I was sent to Ealing College, near Ealing Broadway, for a year. I remember the headmaster's name was MacIntosh and that he had a large white moustache. The school also made an evening visit to the Albert Hall where, resplendent in Eton Collar, I watched a performance of 'Hiawatha' whilst chucking toffee papers into the stalls below.

Owens School, Islington, was the next choice. I even managed to pass the entrance exam and was bought a 5/- Ingersol pocket watch for the effort. Then it was discovered that because of the area we lived in, I did not qualify for a partial grant towards the school's fees and twelve guineas a term was a bit much for father to afford. His income, according to his record of service which I have, was then about six hundred pounds per annum. I was then entered for the Mercers' School, Holborn, entrance exam. I managed to pass and started school there, dressed in new black coat and vest and Arthur Canfor's slightly worn striped trousers. Arthur Canfor's father was manager of Barclays Bank South-Ealing Branch and his son Arthur, being two years older than I, always seemed to grow out of clothes just as I grew into them.

Attending 'Mercers' was one of the really great privileges I have ever been afforded. If I had been asked at the time if it was enjoyable, I expect the answer would have been 'no', but certainly this type of education leading into adulthood was ideal for me.

Mercers was situated in Chancery Lane, High Holborn, opposite the Prudential Building and to get there meant an underground train journey each day. The masters were very strict but fair and "Pride of House and School" was the first lesson to be learned.

Father, by this time, had been moved to 140 Kings Road, Chelsea. A prestigious move, we had to leave our beloved North Acton and move into a house even more to our family liking, 9 Montague Gardens, West Acton. This was about 10 minutes walk from Ealing Common Station and north of the Uxbridge Road. Mary, our maid, was still with us and she adored my brother Alan. I think I was a trial to her.

The family car had meanwhile progressed from the two-seater Bullnose Morris Cowley to a four-seater similar, and then to a four-seater Morris Oxford Saloon. Just before we left North Acton, this in turn gave way to a 1932 Wolseley Hornet Sports Saloon, which was black with a yellow top, fabric body and six cylinders. Father was proud of this car and that year we went to Hemsby, near Yarmouth, for our summer holiday. We met up with my Uncle Cyril's family which consisted of Aunt Maud, 'Hang On' Ken and his eight year old sister Heather. This type of holiday with both families was to be the beginning of many. I was now in my twelfth year and Alan was closing eight.

Becoming a city schoolboy meant a new pattern of behaviour and responsibilities had to be faced up to for the first time. I left home before eight o'clock in the morning, travelled to the City and returned at about 5:00pm. This happened six days a week, as Saturday mornings were Games Days (as were Wednesday afternoons). The school playing fields were at Grove Park in Kent and to arrive there constituted a further hour's journey from the City. On a normal day, travelling from home to school was fairly simple. Leave home, walk for 15 minutes to the station, Piccadilly Line to Holborn, use the escalators, join the Central London Line to Chancery Lane from which station the school was a mere 5 minutes' walk. Any time that a visit to Grove Park was necessitated, the Central Line journey was extended as far as Bank, from whence a walk round the Mansion House to Cannon Street Southern Railway main line soon saw us on a 35 minute journey through New Cross and Lewisham to Grove Park. Here, a brisk 15 minute walk ensured arrival at the ground for a rapid change and on to the field. This ground has now been purchased by The City of London School. I mention this two-hour pretty busy journey twice a week to play a game for no other reason than to point out how much things have changed in 50 years. I can only leave it to the reader's imagination to decide how much. And all for the sake of a game!

But that is how it was. Life was hurried, exciting and everything done with great enthusiasm. Perhaps it was the immediate presence of the City that did this but I prefer to think it was the engendered spirit of School loyalty and House rivalry.

There were four Houses in the school, the history of which went back nearly 500 years. The Houses were Acon, Colet,

Gresham and Whittington. Each name was closely connected with the school; Acon is probably the only name not easily placed. This refers to Thomas a Becket or Thomas of Acon, whose sister Agnes founded the first educational facilities which were later taken over by the Worshipful Company of Mercers. I became a member of Acon and was proud to wear the red flash. I was not destined to be noted for my academic prowess, as my school reports and form placings were always to show, much to my father's chagrin.

Into the field of games, athletics, gym, boxing, debating society and dramatics I hurled myself with great enthusiasm and from the start showed a modicum of above-average success. At the same time, newly arrived, Form IIB gave me a new name.

I had been christened Neville Henry and always answered to that. I was seldom to be referred to as Neville again. Upon receiving one of my first test papers on his desk, a fearsome form master, by the name of 'Lofty' Murray, looked across the form with a searching stare.

"Berryman"? he said.

"Sir", said I, stumbling to my feet from the second row where I had hoped to remain fairly inconspicuous.

"What does the 'N' stand for?" said Murray.

I was not all that fond of my first christian name Neville. Richard, John, Robert or Alan would all have been acceptable. Oh heck, why did my parents have to call me Neville, when I would eventually have to stand up and acknowledge my name in the midst of twenty-nine others of my species in IIB Classroom.

After a few false starts, urged on by some impatient noises from 'Lofty' Murray, I eventually mumbled "Neville, Sir".

"What"? he bellowed

"Neville" I said, a degree louder.

This time he heard, but my embarrassment had alerted the class to the fact that perhaps I had an Achilles' Heel and a roar of laughter greeted the announcement. In the very back row, a lad by the name of Mills, one of the LCC sponsored Brain Children (no fees for them), bellowed "Neville the Devil – Old Nick".

Mills came from East London, of unprivileged parentage I suspected, no decency these chaps. The damage was done however, and I was 'Nick' to all from then on.

My brother arrived at the school four years later with a half-fee scholarship and later a Founders' Scholarship, which pleased my father no end. Alan was immediately christened 'Young Nick', which I considered a great compliment.

Mills became one of my best friends. He was a good footballer, but no boxer, and he belonged to Colet House. The day dawned when I should take my revenge for my temporary humiliation and, at 8 Stone 7 lbs, Mills and I were drawn against one another in the House Boxing Competition. For two years I had regularly boxed for the House and never known defeat. I was good. I would probably kill him and the school knew it. The day of the competition arrived and anxious for a quick win and a knockout, or at least a retirement, I boxed very badly. Mills kept sticking his left hand out, not hurting me, but notching up points. I still couldn't land that KO blow and at the end of the third round the judges' decision was given. Mills' gloved hand was raised in victory and I was defeated. There were two judges, I noticed. One of them was 'Lofty' Murray.

Before I leave my friend Mills, revenge was sweet as I returned from soccer at Grove Park one winter's evening. The lights were low in the carriage and flickering as we tick-tacked our way towards the bright lights of the City. Sports gear cases with our boots strung on the handle outside were placed in the baggage racks above.

The carriage was crowded, the train jerked, and a case and boots landed heavily on Mills' head. Someone got up and put the case back. Five minutes later, as we pulled out of London Bridge, another jerk sent the case cascading down again. Mills furiously grabbed it and hurled it across the carriage at Big Vanhegan who stood laughing his head off by the window. Van dodged swiftly. He could have fielded the case easily as his big hands defended the honour of Mercers' 1st XI goal. He chose to dodge however, and the whole shebang went out of the open window. Mills collapsed in laughter "Who's lost a case?", he gasped through mirth-watered eyes.

"You have", we all chorused.

Each term brought an added bonus of another holiday with cousin Ken. The families had deduced that we got on well together and because of that we youngsters entertained each other, consequently taking the weight off the rest of the family. Alan, four years younger, was not a tearaway and spent many hours quietly at his own pursuits; pen and pencil, paint and crayon were his great interests. From an early age he showed great talent in that direction. As he was to mature, his hitherto reserved humour came more to the fore and I have several of his drawings as a teenager to remind me of the fact.

MEMORIES

Montagu Gardens bring back a lot of happy memories. Mary's domain was the rear part of the house and there unfolded in harmony the everyday life of workaday mummy, workaday Mary, Alan, a black cat and a half collie half pomeranian mongrel dog called Prince. Prince I was fond of but I cannot remember a lot about the cat. As an animal it could be a bit stuffy.

One night I was asked to put the cat through the scullery door for its nightly outing. Before I could close the door, the cat was in again. Twice more I repeated this farce and at last in desperation I hurled out the cat, took a quick gander to see that the propulsion was sufficient and slammed the door. Unfortunately, I forgot to withdraw my head at the same time which resulted in a cut head and lacerated right ear. This was my first lesson in the fact that lack of co-ordination could be extremely dangerous.

When father arrived home from work, mother was seldom to be seen in the kitchen area and the lounge or dining room gave him the haven he so rightly deserved after a day at Chelsea. He usually arrived home about 6:00pm. The kitchen range was usually stoked up, and winter evenings were spent doing cross-word puzzles, listening to the radio and reading. The Champion was my favourite weekly as it fulfilled my imaginative brain in the sporting field. Arthur Askey's Band Waggon, Dick Barton – Special Agent, Henry Hall and his dance orchestra, and I think Tommy Handley's ITMA were all the rage.

Boxing interested me very much and I kept scrap books of the big fights from 1935-1939. I queued up for fighters' autographs and I still have them to this day. A fight between England's Jack Peterson and Germany's Walter Neusel coming over the radio at 9:00pm with an enthusiastic crowd roaring them on, did nothing to endear me further to Mary, as my flashing fists and sparkling footwork sent drying tea towels, clothes horses and cat's dishes scudding across the room. I suspect my brother was not over-impressed either. It must have been a merciful release when summer came and discreet street cricket or roller skate hockey took over. Discreet it had to be, as father would never allow us to play in the street. Cyril and family arrived for a few days each year and we went to their home for about the same amount of time.

Holidays away somewhere were an addition. Christmas was always fun and on Boxing Day evenings, mother, father, Uncle Cyril, and Aunt Maud used to take off, dressed up to the nines for the 'Park Lane Hotel' (one of Barclays' Chelsea customers). Mother, I remember, always looked stunning in her evening gowns and the following morning there was a scrabble by us children for the sophisticated hats and streamers that were brought home.

Everyday life, however went on. I moved into forms III and IV and we moved house to 10 Queen Annes Gardens, Ealing, on the south side of Ealing Common. Mary left us to get married and a daily help took over. The year now was 1936 and I was 14 years of age. It would be an impossible task to mention all the holidays we took, although I remember them all quite well. Better I think to give an insight as to the sort of thing that Ken and I got up to.

The 'Borneo Incident' comes swiftly to mind. 97 College Road, Hereford, was my Uncle Cyril's address and Ken attended Hereford County School, where his main claim to fame was on the rugger field. In the same road lived another relative, who was a

GWR Locomotive driver and it was from him I was to learn the excitement of steam travel. Two trips on the footplate was enough however. Unlike most other boys I was not aiming to be a train driver. Uncle Cyril was the Income Tax Inspector for Hereford and some standards of protocol were required at all times. Ken and I found this 'fetish' difficult to live with, as even on weekend car rides and visits we were expected to 'look nice'.

One Sunday we were both dressed in our Sunday Best ready for a visit to Llantony Abbey, but it was obvious that adult preparation and sandwich making would take a tedious half hour. We begged to be allowed half an hour of freedom from the house on a walk. Threatened with death should we be late, we headed off. Ken would show me his new adventure playground, 'Borneo'. It would be a bit of a dirty expedition, so we would only see where it was and explore another time.

In five minutes flat we had scaled several fences, a few five-barred gates and crossed the odd small stream. The going became more overgrown and forest-like, but we still had 20 minutes left and more was beyond. I kept stopping to give my black shoes a rub up. Dad was a terror for clean shoes and he had polished them himself that morning. Suddenly, a piece of marshy ground was before us. We had better return. Was there anything really interesting on the other side? For Ken, a natural countryman, there was always something interesting on the other side; animals, fish, birds, eggs, frogs and newts were his natural environment. We started to cross the marshy ground, which was all right for Ken, he had wellies on. I should have to give my shoes another rub in a minute. Ken was ahead and my shoes were going to be a problem.

"Hey, give me a piggy-back across this bit" I shouted. Much against his will he returned and hoisted me on his back. Twenty steps later he stopped, and told me to get off as his boot was stuck in mud and he could not take another step until it was free.

"Try harder" I urged, but nothing would induce his boot to leave the cloying mud. His struggle had weakened him and he implored me to get off. The thought of my dad's face seeing my shoes induced me to cling on even tighter. He fell forward onto all fours and I quickly drew my legs up out of the mud and water. By this time his nose was level with the marsh and water. The more he implored me to "Get off you silly bugger" the more I held on. It was then, as has happened so often in my life, that I saw the funny side of the situation. Especially as I was dry and Ken was damn wet. I started to laugh. He chortled. I laughed more and his back began to tremble as he broke into uncontrolled fits of laughter interspersed by watery bubbles. I was nearly helpless with laughter and then it happened. I peed myself. Ken, feeling a strange damp change of temperature in the region of his middle back, hitherto quite dry, gave a snort of disgust, half rose and rolled over.

We got back to 97 College Road five minutes late and a lot later we all arrived at Llantony Abbey.

The families did not meet up for the summer holiday that year. I expect a change was as good as a rest. Instead we went to East Wittering and shared a bungalow with the Precious family.

Mr and Mrs Precious were a well-to-do couple who lived in Gunnersbury Avenue, Ealing. He owned a laundry and their pride and joy was a right little spoilt brat of a daughter by the name of Pamela. I could get by with Mrs P, just. She was very 'girls public school' and treated me like the ruffian she thought I was. Alan fared better. He was the same age as Pamela and discretion has always been one of his attributes.

Naturally I found Pamela a sore trial as she always expected to join in my games. I used to organise cricket matches with the Vicar's party who were living in the adjoining bungalow. A funny lot they were, coming from Erith, a parish in SE London. The fact that the mixture of boys and girls were all good sports and good with a ball was enough to redeem them from all sins in my eyes. Pamela was myopic and always insisted on batting first. We have all met the type. Harold Larwood, in the Test series the following year has been accredited with the first 'Body Line bowling'. I assure you the cricketing records are wrong, and should be amended.

It was thanks to the Vicar that I first came eye to eye with womanhood in the flesh so to speak. One of the boys of the party invited me to join him in the boarded roof space in the bungalow next door. Un-noticed, we secreted ourselves in the roof space adjoining one of the girls dormitories whilst they were out swimming. Breathlessly we awaited their return and soon two of the girls arrived. Our eyes were firmly glued to the knot holes in the boarding. It was a windy day and the draught tearing through those knot holes was gale force. Time stood still. Eventually they stripped and dried off before dressing. My heart pounded and my eye watered. It had taken me 14 years to discover what girls kept covered up, but it was worth it. Thanks Vicar, that was a smashing holiday.

THE CHALLENGE

Dad had a friend in the motor trade in Chelsea. Always a keen motorist, he had to have such friends and it was due to him that I experienced travel at over 100 mph in one of the glorious racing Bugattis. On a weekend visit to Bristol (the farm) Dad, friend and owner Franklin and I burned up the road to the West. My school cap blew off but we didn't stop to look for it. Dad felt like 'Toad' (Poop Poop).

Anyhow, Terry Swinny of Chelsea owned a 1905 Humber Open Tourer and he and Dad shared the driving that winter for the London to Brighton Veteran Car Run. We did well, despite a slipping drive belt and leaking radiator. I was invaluable. Seated in the back I sprinkled resin powder on the drive belt when instructed and constantly chewed gum to stop the leak. It was perishing cold after an 8:00am start from London Bridge and at one stop I was allowed Rum in my hot coffee.

Upon arrival in Brighton we parked and attended a Reception where we were presented with a medal. Step Granddaughter Ruth now has this, given at a time when I distributed my athletic medals to the younger members of the family. I did two Brighton Runs and father continued to drive the car for many years more.

The following spring found us on holiday with Cyril's family again. This time we were at Ogmore near Bridgend, South Wales, and the surrounding hills echoed to our laughter. The bungalow we stayed in stood high on a windswept slope. It had a cellar where wet clothing was dried and Ken and I used to hide away for a quiet smoke if one of us had been crafty enough to snitch a cigarette from a parental pocket. It was fashionable to smoke in 1936 and most adults did so but as now, not so children. The same went for alcohol but this never stopped us having a quick swig and topping the bottle up with water. It was Easter and it was quite cold.

One morning on the rocky coastline with a good half gale blowing I challenged Ken to a run round a high clump of rocks projecting into the sea. As the waves retreated, a clear five feet of sand was exposed on the seaward end of the outcrop before the waves dashed shorewards again covering the whole rock face in terrifying wave and spume. I, being the challenger and to test the practicality of the exercise, was to go first. I watched the pattern of the waves carefully. There was not going to be a lot of time to spare getting round to safety on the other side. Suddenly I was off like a hare. As I reached the end of the projection I saw a huge wave curling towards me, but I was round. Sprinting like the Under-14 100 Yard Champion I was I reached safety high up the beach the other side.

Communication was not easy in a howling wind over a 30 foot high rock while the seas pounded the shore, so after several attempts to inform Ken that it was dead easy I concentrated my gaze on the seaward end of the rocks. Swish, gasp, swish, gasp. The waves roared as they pounded and withdrew. In a moment there he was, my beloved cousin Ken, outlined for a brief second against a background of angry sea and sky before he was spread like a blown piece of paper over the rock face by the biggest wave of the morning. Fortunately he was unhurt, but for being wet he might just have well have done a running jump from the top. He seemed particularly concerned about his new navy blue school raincoat which surprised me I remember, as it had protected him in places.

We hurried back to the safety of our den and gained access to the cellar without detection. There he stripped off in a corner handing me his sodden clothing which I solemnly put through a huge cast iron mangle. The mangle wheels squeaked quite a bit and I had to wind slowly. Suddenly the door at the top of the steps opened. A light was switched on and there stood Aunt Maud. I was 'catched', with a pair of trousers half way through the rollers.

"My God" she cried. "Those are Ken's. Where is he"?

ANNIE

Until 1935 Uncle Cyril's car was a four seater open Bullnose Morris which he affectionately nicknamed 'Annie'. He and Annie were old friends. They had an understanding. She would always continue straight up the road even if he abandoned her steering wheel, an act which he performed in an unsurpassed manner as he turned, knelt on the seat and beat the living daylights out of Ken and I in the rear. I gather we got up his nose sometimes and it was not unknown for us to be abandoned on a country roadside to '... bloody well walk home'. I do not remember ever completing such a walk but we certainly covered a few miles before someone relented and picked us up again.

At such times Aunt Maud did not have quite the faith in Annie that Cyril did and was often observed leaning across to the driving position attempting to interfere with Annie's natural ability. This interference seemed to cause Annie to swing wildly from one side of the road to the other.

One day Annie and Cyril were forced to part, and a brand new Wolseley 12 appeared at Ogmore. There was only one garage and the new Wolseley was reverently garaged, whilst Father's older model stood outside.

I was going through an awkward period at this time. Certainly I did not believe any instructions until it was proved that such information was correct and not just a try on.

Above the new Wolseley on the wall was secured a two foot, six inch red fire extinguisher with those challenging instructions in gold letters "To Operate, Turn Handle to Right and Strike Knob". I turned the handle to the right and struck the knob. Nothing happened. I knew jolly well it wouldn't so I then picked up a spanner and tapped the knob. Jolly swindle these things. People pay a lot of money for such rubbish. There was a half brick behind the Wolseley's front wheel and I gave the useless knob a good thump with it.

All hell was suddenly let loose. Adults get so panicky, don't they? Nobody would get near the fountain of extinguisher fluid, but it finally dribbled to a halt. The car was put outside and Father and Uncle Cyril started washing it. It would appear that the fluid was corrosive. I already had several holes in my shirt and the car washing seemed to go on for days.

That evening the families were destined to visit a fairground at Porthcawl. Has anyone ever been to a fair without going on anything and without any pocket money?

In fact, Mother had suffered inestimable embarrassment at Knightsbridge Underground Station the previous Christmas as I tore up the escalator before her and performed an act I had wished to carry out many times before.

At the top of the escalator I was unobserved as I smashed in the reinforced cardboard on a little red box that was labelled "Break Open and Pull Handle to Stop Escalator". And it did.

Mother, together with other passengers, arrived at the top surprised and walking. Seeing me at the summit looking angelic, she intuitively grabbed my arm and hurried through the ticket barrier.

"You little swine" she hissed, and I hadn't yet said a word, or yet seen Father Christmas, but that year I never did.

Such happy times however, were soon to be marred by family misfortune. Dad was saddened by the death of his father who had been suffering for a year or more with heart troubles. The funeral was shortly before we moved from Acton to Ealing and he was buried in Cefn Cemetery near Merthyr. When Grandma died some 25 years later her ashes were buried with him. He would have been 65, she 87.

Whilst on the subject of Grandma Berryman, she really did live a very pampered life. She was born with a silver spoon in her mouth, and would never countenance personal inconvenience. Spoilt to a degree by her three daughters (but not so much by her sons), she always insisted upon the very best of everything and remained until the end quite immaculate.

A large woman in build, she was extremely autocratic and had been known to wave down and stop the Merthyr-Brecon train with her brolly when it started its journey without her. In their lifetimes my Berryman Grandparents saw little of me, but we were living in times when 150 mile journeys were not entered into lightly. Train and coach travel was very good and reliable, but expense had always to be considered. A factor that seems to have been greatly minimised by ensuing generations.

That year also saw my end as a sprinter but one last chance remained of winning the Junior 100 yards. Sports Saturday arrived and Dad decided to drive to sports day across London. Held up in traffic, we arrived just in time to see my arch-rival Tommy Ninan romp to victory. Previously I had never failed to better Tommy in this event and I was more than put out. The only redeeming feature was that he also was Acon House, but we could have had points for 1st and 2nd and the Cock House Championship hinged on the athletics. Such was the strong House feeling within Mercers.

Recently there has been much controversy in the field of Education relating to the worth or advisability of competition in schools. In my opinion the non-competition lobby want their heads examining. In my day every competitor was admired and encouraged and even loved for his or her efforts and the losers were never demeaned. So enthusiastic were Boat Race Crews, that to celebrate Victory, they often used to dip their Cox into the river.

TO KILL A CAT

On a visit to East Wittering that year, 1936, I stood on the stony beach with my dog Prince beside me and watched the new Cunard Queen Mary (83,000 tonnes) sail on her maiden voyage to the United States. Evening walks across the golden corn fields to Itchenor were a regular pursuit, with refreshment obtained mid-walk at Itchenor's riverside pub. In mid-summer, if one saw thirty people there I should be surprised. Now, one of the South of England's major yachting centres, three thousand visitors would be nearer the mark, and all in 50 years.

In the closing days of the year 1936 King Edward VIII abdicated and this was also to be a tragic year for our family. During mid-winter in cold London we were horrified to learn that Cyril and Maud's daughter, Ken's sister, had skated on the River Wye at Hereford on her evening return home from school. She was with several friends as the ice broke.

Her friends were fortunately rescued, but Heather was washed under the ice and remained missing for 6 weeks until the thaw, when her body was recovered many miles from the scene of the tragedy. It was a long time before I was to see Uncle Cyril smile again. He adored his daughter and never got over the loss.

I have previously mentioned that sprint competitions were now pretty well finished for me – Donald Vanhegan was proving impossible to beat in any of the shorter distances as well as long and high jumps. He was later to be a London Public Schools Athletic Champion and a Colet man to boot. There had to be a way back to the medal ceremony.

About now I learned that there were several ways to kill a cat and learned the art of gamesmanship. Van did not run 440, School Handicap 660 or the 880 yards. This surely was the way to combat the problem. Unfortunately, my age group contained several quite talented chaps at these distances, but by all manner of ploys, victory was to be mine eventually in all these events.

Being almost a sprint, the 440 was the difficult one, and in 1938 the chips were really down. I hardly stood a chance against the opposition. To make matters worse I was now Intermediate House Captain responsible for Middle and Junior Schools and answerable to God's right-hand man, my Senior House Captain. I thought about the coming race a great deal as it was just about all I could win that year. Second and third places meant little to me, although I never minded losing.

Sports Day dawned. This time, I arrived early, and we lined up for the 440 yards. 'Bang' went the gun. I set off at full lick, and I mean flat out. The first bend I had a lead of 10 yards and half way down the back straight I must have been 40 yards clear. The opposition must have been demoralised. The only snag was, I was done. There was not a lot left, the blood pounded in my ears and I was beginning to reel with the strain. With 100 yards to the finishing line my vision started to blur, my legs were leaden and my chest heaved painfully. All the while my adversaries were closing the gap, and the green, yellow and blue of the other House Colours were intermingling with the Acon red – I crossed the tape completely blind and stumbled to the side of the track. As sound and vision returned to my shattered body, I felt a hand on my shoulder. I looked up to see my House Master, bluff G G Allen. He relaxed his grip on my shoulder and smiled as he said two magic words.

"You won!," adding "and I'll tell you another thing my lad – you will never die in bed."

I think it probable that I will not. The good Lord has many ways in which to kill his cats off.

Brother Alan had joined Mercers the previous year, and 'Young Nick' ceased being a brother and became a valued member of Junior House. Alan was a big chap for his age, goodness knows why. By the time we were in our twenties the physical difference between us had re-balanced and today he is the leaner of the two of us and I am delighted to say he has ceased being a junior and has gained full brotherly status.

At that time however, he was to be an invaluable sporting member of the House. Not naturally inclined to push himself forward, he had to be bullied into competing. Whereupon he showed considerable ability at many events and the family were very proud.

As a boxer he was not likely to be terribly useful, as wearing spectacles was hardly conducive to the sport. Acon was short of a 7 stone 6lb competitor in the House competition. It had to be death or glory for him.

He complained bitterly that he could not easily see his opponent without his specs let alone hit him. In three easy lessons I taught him all I knew of the gentle art. I decided that the only way he could win was to prod away with his left glove until he sensed the foe was near enough to clobber with his right.

"What happens if he lets go at the same time?" he queried.

"Don't bother about things like that" I said, "Just get on with it."

Of course he won, but I do not think he ever donned the gloves again.

Family life at home was unknowingly enjoying the last 18 months of peace. Dad was enjoying his Freemasonry and Motoring, Mum was running the house like clockwork, Alan was progressing well in his scholastic studies but I was not giving my father much confidence in that direction. What he "would do with me" was his constant concern. I had thoughts on that subject too but I did not say a lot as the subject distressed my mother. If I could pass the exams required I would join the Fleet Air Arm.

I made one further visit to Grandmother Berryman, visiting Aunt Topsy in Bristol on the way. She and her husband Herbert entertained me well and did all manner of things to make my stay interesting. They even allowed the household to be roused at

4:00am one morning in order to listen on the radio to the blow by blow account of the Joe Louis and Tommy Farr World Heavyweight fight in the USA. It was a magnificent fight. Louis was almost defeated. Farr took British boxing to the highest peak it had ever attained in the Heavyweight Class.

The following week, Britain was agog with excitement as the fight film was shown at the cinema. By then I had moved on to Grandmother's in Merthyr. Newly-widowed and in her regal finery, she was enticed to the local 'flea pit' to see the film. Excitement ran at fever pitch in Merthyr that evening. Merthyr was only a valley-width apart from Tonypandy, Farr's home village, and the audience rose to his 15-round bid for the World Championship as a man. The cinema rocked and I, never renowned for lack of enthusiasm, rocked with them. Poor Grandmother, who did not know a gum shield from a jock strap, sat bemused and not a little ruffled, as I was wont to bash peoples' hats in sometimes out of sheer exuberance. For me it became an unparalleled boxing occasion. As for Grandmother, well she never stopped mentioning it for the rest of her days, so it must have done something for her.

Dad sometimes took me to the Stadium Club in Holborn. He was a good Dad as I do not think he enjoyed boxing overmuch himself. I was so obviously enthused that we used to sit at the supper tables around the ring enjoying the very best of food and wine (his boys were always allowed a small glass) whilst the up and coming boxers of the year pounded away at each other. He was always amused at the amount of food I could pack away on these occasions. I was no fool. It was better than egg on chips with Mother in Lyons Corner House whilst on a shopping expedition.

Uncle Ernie too, was coming in for the odd bit of hat bashing, for whilst accompanying me to a Middlesex versus Surrey match I would be reasonably restrained, (apart from 3 sixes in 3 balls from Big Jim Smith and 98 from Patsy Hendren at Lords one day).

A Saturday at Craven Cottage with Fulham at their best, could be a different matter. Ernie always referred to me as 'Henryman' due to the fact that whilst being taught to remember my name and address I used to gabble:

"My name is Neville Henryman Threeuneranleven Norend Road."

The system of communication obviously worked, as I was always safely returned to my distraught mother when lost.

When I showed a little too much exuberance on sporting occasions with Ernie he used to say quietly and unsmilingly "Henryman! Must you?". I will always be grateful to Ernie for his interest in me. A great sportsman himself, he taught me to love games outside of my own active involvement.

JUST A STONE'S THROW

In 1938 Ken came to London to work for Barclays Bank. He lived with us at Queen Annes Garden for a month before he found digs. Employed at the Northfields branch, he stuck the job out until war released him from his misery. Never a natural at such an occupation, I remember he was always at odds with some senior member of staff or another and his pet hate was balancing the postage stamp book; which he never could, which could explain why he is a very successful businessman today I suppose.

Ken's employment in London was a bonus for both of us. I was able to introduce him to more of my townee ways and he became a great companion. Alan was four years younger than I and at 16 years of age that was quite a lot when considering like interests.

I was now beginning to get interested in the opposite sex, amateur dramatics and adventurous cycle journeys. Camping also interested me and Easter of that year took four school friends and me to Clymping near Arundel for a camping week. Cycle was our mode of transport and the destination was the Vicar of Clymping's orchard. I have always had a great affinity with Vicars. Seventy miles was a fair distance to cycle in one day, but our equipment was minimal and by today's standards, unsuitable. However, we camped, swam and hiked and returned after a week.

On the journey home, at Dorking, one of my friends was unable to keep his pedal on the crank as the threads were worn. He decided to go home by train but as far as I was concerned that was not on. Together we had started, together we would finish. How to do that was a difficult question. With an obstinacy now well known to my family, I decided it could be done. I removed my own crank and pedal from my fixed wheel cycle and fitted it to his free wheel cycle.

"... and how will you manage?" he asked

"Don't worry about that," I said, "just damn well get on with it".

I rode from Dorking to Ealing with one pedal. When and only when, my friends had departed with their bikes via London transport for their respective homes, I was very physically sick – I never told a soul, of course.

I was never a good cricketer, but that summer I made the third XI school team and won the 880 yards on Sports Day. The family holiday that year was to be at Stone on the River Blackwater and my school report was terrible, as usual.

Stone was an exciting venue. We rented a fisherman's cottage, one of six, with a hundred square yards of private joint front garden leading directly to the estuary. It was there, just coming up to sixteen that I learned a lot more about other people.

The other five families adjoining us were all very much family people with a similar background to our own. With fifteen or sixteen teenagers amongst the party, I remember an idyllic holiday. Even Ken joined us for a week.

It was from Stone that I first sailed a dinghy. With a minimum of instruction I set off Westwards to Osea Island and was picked up by Father in his car four hours later at Burnham on Crouch five miles to the East.

Tides had entered my life. My 6 foot 3 inch pal, Buster Sharpe, was a magnificent swimmer and everyone knew he would win the two hundred yards freestyle event at Maldon regatta week.

We all turned out to witness 'Buster's' unquestionable win, although the standard was very high. It was an evening event and the taped-off distance of water was grey in the diminishing light. Suddenly our hopes were dashed. The event was to be cancelled. The rules required a minimum of six swimmers and there were only five.

The officials were somewhat bemused as I left the spectators enclosure, stripped off to my underpants and lined up with the best of Essex. Buster won in a record time for the event. Five minutes later using a mixture of side, back and breaststroke I too crossed the finishing line to resounding cheers from the spectators. We went home triumphant, with the biggest challenge cup I had yet to see.

Not to put too dramatic a point on it, we could sense that all was not well in the political world. Chamberlain had returned from his meeting with Hitler. 'Peace in our Time' was his announcement and my Father was relieved but not convinced. Amongst senior boys at school there was talk of joining the reserve forces. For me, I was not concerned in the slightest.

The year of 1939 was to be my School Certificate Year. My Maths and French were well below par and extra tuition was the order of the day. The school play that year was The Imaginary Invalid (Le Malade Imaginaire). I had always taken girls' parts in school productions and I was cast as Toinette, the invalid's maidservant. An amusing part and I enjoyed doing it.

Within a very short time of finishing The Invalid I was asked by The Old Mercers Dramatic Company if I would play the part of Bimbo in their production of Ian Hay's The Housemaster. It was not a very demanding part and the production was to be at the Cripplegate Theatre. I agreed to do the part but in retrospect I think my exam revision suffered as a result. Mother and Father attended the theatre one evening and knowing them as I did they would have been very proud of my selection as Bimbo. In the play I had to ask my sister (smashing piece she was too) if she "... had a piece of chocolate". She (Buttons) produced a piece of from her knicker leg. "You haven't got a cold piece I suppose" was my rejoinder.

Sports Day came and went. Unable to train very much due to study, the best I could do was a poor third in the 880, whilst my brother Alan redressed the Berryman 'support for Acon' balance with several successful results.

My first introduction to light entertainment came with a Music Hall Evening in the school hall. Friend Tony Barbour and I gave a mind reading act as our main contribution to the performance. Blindfolded, he had to know what I held in my hand, when borrowed from the audience.

"Now this TIME I have here. Now WATCH your answers, don't hurry, don't take any wrists, I mean risks."

This sort of entertainment was regarded with a modicum of suspicion by the Mercers establishment, but in a way the slightly relaxed standards were to help prepare us for getting along with all types which became so very important in the war years to follow.

Until then we had circulated entirely in the London Public School environment. Dear Old Mills was the odd man out but he had a fine character which was proved when I boxed with him at ten stone. He was very brave to even get into the ring. I had been studying Tommy Farr's tactics for two years.

I was now playing soccer for the 1st XI as inside forward. Bert White, an Arsenal player, was coaching some of us for the London Public Schools XI. I was very proud when he complimented me on my ability to shoot low and hard, but I was not chosen to represent London Public Schools.

One Sunday Father took the family to his new Motor Club at Sydenham. It was to be a Sports Day. Father was proud of his Citroen Light 15, Registration Number DLK 121. It had a throaty roar and rapid acceleration.

In his mind there could only be one winner in the sledge race and I, being very good at gymnastics was to be his jockey. We held a hurried discussion on tactics and I was attached by rope and surf board to the rear of Father's pride and joy. We were off. The grass was golden, shiny and hard. When we reached the end of the course we rounded a post for the return journey. The Citroen, with plus-foured and capped Reg at the wheel, was just ahead. With eyes glued to the course he never attempted to slow for the turn and went round in a sharp arc. Momentum threw me wide and with a slack rope I came right up alongside the car as father, with a flourish, stuck in a lower gear for a rapid return up course.

Foresight is a wonderful attribute and I began to holler. The Bank Manager never even glanced in my direction. With a snap the rope tensioned and up went the board, and I with it, backside over top. As I raised myself painfully from the grass I saw the black Citroen, board and rope (still bouncing) disappear into the dust.

Arriving at the winning post ahead of all others, Reg was convinced he had won. Upon being told he was disqualified as his jockey had fallen off, he was heard to remark "Good God, is my car all right?"

The end of term arrived. I had not done well in my exam and I should have to take it again at Christmas. However, it was then decided that I should leave school, and it was a sad parting that late July day in 1939 as I bade my friends, amongst whom were nearly all the Masters, farewell.

The return to Stone on holiday was fun, but blighted by the worry of the political situation. Hutton, Compton and Edrich were serving England well in the Test Cricket series, and Bradman was still the big name for Australia.

Ken arrived for a week and all the usual competitions and games were engaged in. Gymnastics I loved.

"Make some backs," I shouted to a couple of girls. As they knelt down, with a dive I was over them and with a forward roll was on my feet.

"I'll do three," said Ken.

"Four," said I.

"Five," he continued.

"Six," I said.

When we decided eight was enough, I went first and cleared the eight kneeling ladies, just clipping the last one, and was again on my feet.

Ken pounded up the long run, took off a bit soon, sent himself and the last kneeler flying and staggered to his feet clutching his neck. He looked a bit pale which was not surprising as he'd broken his collar bone. Much to family relief this was to be our last holiday together.

WAR – 1939

Poland was invaded. My birthday was 1st September and we were to return home with masked headlamps on 2nd September. The Army was encamped in an adjoining field and I felt sorry for the deprivations they were enduring. I had befriended two young soldiers and rose early to take them hot water to shave. I stumbled as I was crossing the field and dropped a scalding kettle on my ankle and foot. I had been very helpful to the Army and in appreciation for my efforts they took me along to the local cottage hospital where I was welcomed with opened arms at 6:45 in the morning.

Sunday 3rd September I remember gathering 'en famille' in the dining room at Queen Annes Gardens around the radio.

At eleven in the morning Prime Minister Neville Chamberlain would speak to the Nation. His memorable speech is well known, with his closing words...

"In consequence, we are at War with Germany."

*With a snap the rope tensioned and up went the board, and I with it,
backside over top. As I raised myself painfully from the grass I saw the black
Citroen, board and rope (still bouncing) disappear into the dust.*
*Arriving at the winning post ahead of all others, Reg was convinced he had
won. Upon being told he was disqualified as his jockey had fallen off, he was
heard to remark "Good God, is my car all right?"*

I ventured a quick glance towards my Father, probably for reassurance. He was looking straight out of the window and tears were streaming down his face. Britain was at War.

THE LITTLE BROWN HAT

Sunday 3rd September 1939 was a sad day for the World and we were to be embroiled in a war of many nations for the next six years.

At 11:15am we, 'what was gathered there below', were hardly surprised when the air raid sirens started to wail, and I am quite sure we expected to hear the sound of falling bombs and the CRUMP CRUMP we later got to know only too well. It turned out to be a false alarm and we set about our everyday jobs. Mother seldom failed to cook a roast on Sunday and I expect it was already in the oven. Father nipped off with the car for half a pint and Alan probably to his pen and paper. For me it was back to my bike. It was a very old bike and needed constant attention and sub-sidising from the family budget, but it was the real interest in my life.

Normally I reserved Saturday for the removal of any parts requiring attention. Saturday it had to be as often the operation went on until Sunday by which time, if unfinished, a further week elapsed before I was able to do the odd 'wheelie' up and down Queen Annes Gardens. My favourite work spot was immediately outside the back door.

On reflection this was probably due to the fact that, just as now, if I do a job I have to involve others. I am happy enough to do the job myself, but all and sundry should enjoy it also. I had a captive audience in Mother as she spent a lot of time in the kitchen but she was always complaining about spoons with bent handles. Anyone who has ever had a bike in the family has spoons with bent handles.

Alan had a bicycle too, but I seem to remember him using it with reluctance. He always seemed to walk everywhere; a pursuit which obviously gave him time to think about what he would do upon arrival at his destination. A matter that concerned me little; 'get there quickly and think about it later' was for me an attitude which typifies the difference in character between us. I am happy to say the years have slowed me down a little and I no longer use a bike.

There was little doubt that the population of Britain were in shock and we went about wondering what to do for the best. Some businessmen with expensive stocks were obviously worried. Valerie, later to be my wife, recalls that her father, who was in the motor business, sold off his entire stock of new cars at little or no profit, just to get money in and pay off the overdraft at the bank.

It was a 'Let us sit on the fence for a while' time. Soon, when people realised that sudden death was not around the corner we resumed a more normal life, and we youngsters soon forgot about the trauma and carried on as usual.

Normally I would have spent the next three months doing private study and taking tuition in order to take my Matriculation again at Christmas. In those days one had to pass with a "credit" rating in six subjects to obtain the Matriculation Grade. Six passes would give a General School Certificate. It was an all or nothing situation and I was not looking forward to it. The Fleet Air Arm was still my choice of career so I had to pass to get in. Now with a war and the reserve forces being called up there was a desperate need of men and women to take their places in civilian life.

What should I do? The question concerned the whole family. The future was unforeseeable and, with compulsory service inevitable anyway, it was decided I should go out to work in the wide wide world. I wished to be independent of my Father's considerable influence in the world of business and, full of my own importance, I departed to Shell Mex House on the Embankment to inform them that they needed me and that I could start anytime. My interviewer thought otherwise however, and felt that Shell had enough problems on their hands at the moment thank you, but they would let me know. A few days elapsed and I heard nothing and, not given to sitting around, I went to see the

Personnel Manager of Unilever at their Blackfriars office, all to no avail.

The Daily Mail nearly got a new junior reporter, but changed their minds when they saw my essay on 'The Future of British Merchant Shipping'. Well, it was something to do with shipping anyway, and I must admit I had no great ideas on the subject.

A long week passed before I finally approached my Dad. Did he think that perhaps Barclays Bank could use my banking experience. After all, I had heard my Father accept and refuse overdrafts, I had regularly carried the Branch coinage up and down to the strong room and knew how to open and close the formidable doors of several of their branches. I thought my Father might have had a few misgivings as he agreed to have a word with the staff manager. His misgivings were not without foundation, it should be remembered that Cousin Ken was already somewhat insecurely ensconced at Barclays Northfields.

Shortly afterwards a letter arrived from Barclays Head Office addressed to Mr N H Berryman and offering me an interview. Then and there my Father started to brief me on how to conduct myself.

A reasonable grey suit I did possess and with the old school tie and well polished shoes he would allow me to attend the Holy of Holy's, 54 Lombard Street, London EC1. An address indelibly imprinted on my brain. One problem however, I did not possess a hat, and a hat was imperative.

After meeting my Father at the office the following Monday, I was allowed to drive the Citroen home, no 'L' plates in those days, and this was the way I was taught to drive. From Chelsea to Kensington, down Holland Park into Shepherds Bush, Acton Vale and home. On this journey I was told to stop the car in Shepherds Bush. We got out, nobody ever locked a car in 1939, and walked across to Dunn's shop. Once inside I saw several hats I could perhaps take to, but suddenly Father spotted a bargain, and if Father spotted a bargain it had to be got.

From the start I did not like the brown trilby with broad darker brown ribbon, priced at the greatly reduced figure of 4s 6d. It was a relief to find that it was too small.

A little tight perhaps, but he knew how to fix that, and he and the salesman decided that the hat was eminently suitable and such a bargain to boot.

Once at home and after our meal, Father sat quietly before the fire performing with the hat. He warmed it, he kneaded it, he gently stretched it and he warmed it again. When he had been at this for some twenty minutes, I was bidden to sit on the stool at his feet. I obeyed, and that hat was warmed once again.

It had a leather inner band, and without warning the hat was withdrawn from the warmth of the glowing coals and literally rammed about my ears. I yelled with pain as the leather band, red hot, met my forehead. It was on so tightly I couldn't quickly get it off. Later the family unanimously decided that the hat fitted.

I went for the interview. Mr Fisher, the Staff Manager, liked me. He also probably liked my hat, after all its not every day a chap with a halo imprinted on his crown asks for a job.

A week later, still in September, I was asked to present myself to Mr Arthur Jarvis at Barclays Melbury Court Kensington Branch. A very prestigious post, as only the elite of society banked there.

Brother Alan meanwhile had returned to Mercers but there was talk of evacuation to the sister school Collyers at Horsham in Sussex. We hoped that the situation would not get serious enough to warrant that, and at the moment there was no sign of a war escalation. Poland was occupied but France stood firm, a bastion between England and the enemy. Air activity was negligible by both sides and the British Army was slowly making its way into France. We had a short sharp reminder that we were vulnerable when HMS Royal Oak was sunk at anchor in Scapa Flow by a U-Boat. We were constantly aware that our merchant shipping was at peril, but I shall not dwell on the history of the war as so much information is available on that subject. I shall instead attempt to tell the story of how war affected our family, and some of their adventures.

AFFAIRS OF THE HEART

Christmas time at the Bank was very busy, situated as it was midway between the big shops of Kensington High Street and Olympia (where Bertram Mills Circus was a great attraction). Masses of change used to pass over the counter, but as yet I was not to be trusted anywhere near the customers.

The staff were few in number, and we only ever referred to each other by surname. Mr Jarvis, the Manager, a bachelor of 55 years of age, had seen some service in Barclays Dominion Colonial and Overseas in Milan. He was an interesting man with a lot of charm, just the character for Melbury Court. Mr Fairs was the Chief Cashier, Mr Davis the Security Clerk, Mr Grieves the Ledger Clerk, Miss Gould the shorthand/typist and I the Junior. I had to arrive at 8:30am and get the show on the road. It went unsaid that the others would arrive in order of seniority before 9:00am.

Mr Jarvis would arrive to suitable humble greetings at 9:15am. It was enjoyable work and without a war getting in the way, I think I should have stayed with banking. The work being of a routine nature suited me well, as over the years I have come to realise that underneath a flamboyant exterior I hide a fairly mundane character. I am good therefore at routine tasks at which, once confident, I have the happy knack of cutting the corners and frills from. In consequence the job appears to be simple to the onlooker.

This ability has served me no good whatsoever as either no credence is given to my ability or else more work arrives on my doorstep. I have never had many bosses in life but I even treat myself in the same way.

I got on well with the staff and my approach to my job somewhat amused Arthur Jarvis the manager. He certainly kept me up to scratch and was swift to criticise if I transgressed, but once the doors were shut for the afternoon, he was a friendly and humorous man.

It was inevitable that I became enamoured by a few of the smart young ladies who arrived to conduct business, and if I had my head down and missed one of my favourites he would often give me a nudge and a knowing wink, which very often covered me in confusion and bought a few blushes from the other side of the counter.

One pretty girl who was an assistant at Madam Lenze, the fashion shop in Melbury Court, was a bit overpainted and not too well educated but I took her to the cinema several times and finally took her home to tea. Mother looked down her nose somewhat, although outwardly charming. My Father was non-committal. Our friendship however lasted the whole time I was in Kensington.

Another little affair was with the bank cleaner's daughter and she was a 'raver'. I did not take her home, as Father might not have been non-committal. Our typist, Miss Gould, a 25 year old blue stockinged spinster, sensed my little dalliances and took every opportunity to reproach me.

"Berryman" she would say, "you should be more interested in your work." But then she didn't know how interesting the cleaner's daughter was when she was cleaning the basement.

The impression I am trying to convey about this period (1939-40), is that to me it was something and nothing. Certainly the odd poor chap was being killed somewhere but considering there was a war on it was hardly enough to be noticed. Kensington High Street was thriving and I could still get a three course lunch for 1s 3d (6p in today's currency). Half a pint of beer was 4d in the Saloon Bar. A usual lunch for me was a glass of milk (2d) and a ham roll (4d). I could exist quite well therefore on 2s 6d all the week if I cycled to work, and I gave mother 15s for my keep at home. The remaining 12s 6d went on cinemas, YMCA subscription and financing the purchase of two tailor-made suits at five guineas each.

Before Easter 1940 I developed jaundice and was poorly for a while, after which my Dad insisted I went to Hastings for a week's convalescence, and he paid the bill.

The Royal Air Force had taken over some large hotels in Hastings and had installed No. 1 Initial Training Wing. I watched the young sergeants at their training. Little did anyone know that by the following Christmas many of them would be dead, swallowed up by the Battle of Britain or the immediate aftermath. I was still determined to join the Fleet Air Arm when I could.

What I did in a small Hastings hotel for a week I shall never know. I do have a photograph of that time, looking the picture of health with a small Woolworths football in one hand. The habit of Mercers playground football died hard it appeared. I fell in love with the chambermaid, but returned to Ealing still pure white.

BLITZ

Home again and with the onset of summer, weekends were spent with friends and going cycle riding. We usually went towards Esher and Leatherhead. Ken was one of the gang and the Surrey lanes heard much of our laughter. We were very happy.

Father was not so happy as he found his petrol ration did not go too far when used on his Citroen. He sold it and purchased a 1938 Ford 10. He never liked the car, sold again and bought a Standard 9.

In May the Country woke up with a start. The Germans had made rapid advances towards the Channel Coast. The Maginot Defence Line was by-passed, Belgium overrun and Allied Forces pushed back to the beaches. The next month is history and after the Dunkirk evacuation from France, Britain stood alone, and for the first time we all realised it.

Almost immediately the Germans started attacks on our forward air fields in order to gain air superiority. The Royal Air Force fought back with all they had. Prime Minister Chamberlain had stood down and Winston Churchill was leading a Coalition Government. Churchill was the man for the moment. The British people admired him and his speeches were a tremendous encouragement to fight back.

The Local Defence Volunteer force had recently been formed as a civilian part-time army, and later they were to be renamed The Home Guard. Father immediately joined and learnt his rifle drill again.

Alan had been evacuated with the school to Horsham. My friends from the YMCA began to disappear to the forces. I was now seventeen years and nine months of age and mother was anxious that I did not volunteer until I was eighteen. With only a few months to go I decided to keep my head down and keep the peace.

There was just time to take confirmation classes in church, and Ken and I were confirmed together. Most Sundays we managed to go to church. It was due to this church-going that I met Betty who lived in Church Road, South Ealing, near my Father's local pub, The Rose and Crown.

My friend from the YMCA, Frank Ellis, and I both took a shine to this little bright-eyed mouse of a girl, so we did the honourable thing and shared her. An arrangement which worked very well until he and Ken went off, about the same time, to join the RAF.

While all this was going on, the YMCA had formed a concert party, the purpose of which was to entertain locally based troops. Frank was an excellent pianist, so he became part of the four-piece band and played the odd solo. Another friend, Ray Norman, and I both by nature were natural mimics so we set up an impressionist act. A tap dancer called Audrey taught me to play the ukulele properly, a pastime I had been messing about with for a year or so. We put on a few good performances and of course the acts got more polished as we went along. Ken was still somewhere around, and he did anything I could inveigle him into. I remember one song he took part in, "Three Land-ladies We, What Have Seen Better Days", used to bring the house down. The audiences were terrific of course, bored soldiers will support anything. I used to compere the show, an obvious choice, as, just as I write, I am seldom stuck for a word.

That October in 1940, the Battle of Britain was over, no more contrails over Southern England for a while, but the night bombing began. This was an horrific period for the large industrial cities and London got its fair share. Ealing is one of the Western suburbs of London but the Docks of Eastern London, well marked by the River Thames, were the main targets and the bombing was far from accurate. The Germans had learnt that England was not a healthy place to fly over in daylight and consequently most of the raids were under cover of darkness.

Steel shelters had been provided for families that wanted them and these were erected in gardens. The majority of people however managed by taking cover under the staircase or using public shelters. The London Underground system was packed after 4:00pm, and (if I were not cycling) by the time I was leaving work the platforms below ground were already filling up. Sleeping places were staked out for the night. Families and friends were together, food and drinks were taken and on the whole a jolly atmosphere prevailed. Above ground, Restaurants and Theatres did a roaring business and even at the worst times the eating house always managed to put some sort of Menu together. Whale Steak was quite usually offered or sometimes Horse meat. The Variety Theatre was particularly popular and the Crazy Gang at the London Palladium shows were always my favourite.

Sometimes between leaving work and arriving the next morning a block of shops or a church would be razed to the ground, and the Rescue Services toiled endlessly night after night. The odd chunk of body could often be seen protruding from the rubble and timber but I never remember being the slightest bit afraid for my own life.

Some evenings walking up to the YMCA the uneven drone of German aircraft and their Jumo engines would be interspersed by a long whistle and a thump, which caused the ground to shudder. The searchlights would be scanning the sky and the anti-aircraft guns, usually situated on local parks and commons, would be firing with the distinctive staccato 'crack'. The shrapnel would be heard thudding into the ground nearby and we used to huddle closer to the walls and keep walking.

The YMCA was just right for my leisure time. Most indoor games could be played and there was always the gym for a workout. Someone then had a bright idea and a temporary amalgamation with the YWCA was brought about. This opened up the world a bit for my youthful circle of friends, as for 6d we could dance and have tea and coffee on a Saturday evening.

Betty was a member of the YWCA and we cemented our friendship. It was here I met Elsa, who was a tall German Jewess and what she was doing in the Christian Association the Lord alone knows. However, she was there, and twice a week for a year I met and socialised with her. She had escaped from Germany just before war broke out and previously had been in hiding from the Gestapo. Long before the people of England knew the stories we know today, I heard of the atrocities for myself. Her story was hard for us to understand in our reasonably comfortable world but it made us all the more determined that the war should be won.

SIGN 'ERE

A mixed, tented encampment at Denham in a riverside pasture was to be my holiday that year and it was all good clean fun. The Spitfires from nearby Northolt constantly droned overhead and Betty's sister fell in love with a charming Polish Fighter Pilot named Olik serving with 303 Squadron. I myself was to cross swords with the same squadron two years later.

It was a lonely time, as my best chums had departed and I couldn't wait to join them. At the Bank I was taking my turn on fire watching duties, as well as at home. Two nights every week meant, at the very least, two hours tramping the streets in case fire bombs fell. Sometimes they did and teams of us would rush into action with stirrup pumps and buckets. The docks were often ablaze and it was possible to read a paper at night by the glow in the sky eight miles away. All house windows were taped across to minimise shattering and sandbag-filling was a regular pastime. Dad was trying to grow tomatoes and Mother did her best with the meagre rations. After six months away Alan returned from evacuation at

Horsham and from there on Mercers School was split, half in London and half in Horsham. In order to do his bit, Alan took his turn on fire watch duties and joined the Army Cadet Force which was on a war time footing.

The nearest Barclays Melbury Court got to being destroyed was when one afternoon I was despatched to the Strong Room together with an elderly but elegant lady. Her wish was to remove some silver from her lodged box. I found the box, which was a large packing case, cut the seal and string and stood by while she removed some pieces. Upon conclusion it was my job to re-tie and re-seal the top. I tended to be a bit wholesale with the sealing wax and tapers, and this time I overdid it. The whole damn box of straw and paper caught alight. Panic Stations. After the Auxiliary Fire Service had declared the area safe and all was returned to normal, Miss Gould was heard to say "Berryman is very careless".

Arthur Jarvis replied "That, is the understatement of the Year." In the whole war, I cannot remember being more scared.

It seemed a long winter and before Christmas we were heading up the new ledgers. This required copper-plate writing on the top of each customer's page, a laborious task carried out each year end and much attention was paid to one's work by senior staff. The New Year of 1941 arrived and the war was not going well for Britain and the Commonwealth. The only allies we had were the gallant chaps who had escaped from their occupied countries – French, Poles, Czechs, Norwegians, Dutch, Belgians and there were not a lot of them. The war in the Near and Far East was going particularly badly and we were in reverse gear on every front.

One lunch time in March I asked if I could take a slightly longer lunch hour as I had to get to Acton and back, a journey of four miles. Permission granted I sped off and arrived only to find that my destination, The Royal Navy Recruitment Office, had a large notice pinned to the door "Closed for Lunch – Back at 2 O'clock".

I was distraught, Mr Jarvis would never allow another long lunch break, not even to win the war. I remember standing there feeling quite crestfallen when my eye fell upon an open door down the corridor, outside of which stood a sandwich board marked ROYAL AIR FORCE with directional arrows.

"Oh, Sod the Navy, that will do", I muttered.

Taking the King's Shilling was simple enough. I filled in a form stating my preference of occupation and I noticed that Pilot, Navigator and Wireless Operator/Air Gunner were bracketed under the one heading of Aircrew. I signed as bidden "'ere and 'ere" and before I had fully realised the implication of the act, found myself astride my faithful cycle heading towards Kensington again. Three years of thought, planning and boasting, all gone in ten minutes. No longer could I envisage myself in navy blue and gold braid. No more to imagine the thump of aircraft wheels returning to a storm tossed aircraft carrier. No more the excitement of arriving in foreign parts where I knew that all the nice girls loved a sailor.

Well there it was, the deed was done, I glanced down at the small silver plated badge reposing in my left lapel and I read RAFVR. Oh well I expect I shall look just as well in light blue.

"Sorry Sir, a bit late I know Sir. Yes, Miss Gould, I will get some more stamps before 4 O'clock."

Oh Blimey, I can't wait.

The next three months were very busy and I found myself more and more without the company of my male friends as they left for the Services.

I dearly wanted a motor cycle and had seen the very thing outside a shop in Acton Vale. The price (seven pounds and ten shillings) seemed astronomical and it was, when I earned one pound and ten shillings a week. Each evening I passed the shop and gazed longingly at the much worn adorable machine. How to get the money was the question. The Lord has never allowed me to ponder too long on any problem and he came up with the answer as usual.

A few days later I passed the local big cinema The Globe Acton High Street and across the front was a hoarding "Local Talent Competition – First Prize seven pounds. Second and Third Prizes five pounds and three pounds." I was aware that Ray Norman and

I could hold an audience for a twenty minute spot with the concert party but, as I could not afford to share any cash prize that might come along, I would have to do it alone. I signed "'ere and ere'" once again agreeing that I would duly appear on the Saturday Night.

I do not remember a great deal about my performance. The microphone system was excellent and I relied heavily upon that. I thought a stand up comedian with a funny little hat was very good and would take some beating. He did and I got Second Prize.

Clasping my five pound note I was immediately consumed with ambition to make money the easy way and within a fortnight I had contracted to appear in a similar competition at the Gaumont Hammersmith (now renamed The Odeon) and once again got into the money, Third Prize this time, but it was a bigger competition and another fiver lined my pocket.

I hardly dared tell Father that I wanted a motor bike as I knew he disapproved of them, so the next Monday evening I went along just to look at the thing. On the spot where it had stood for some weeks or more there now reposed a more modern machine priced at thirty pounds and enquiries confirmed my worst fears. My heart's desire had been sold. It took me days to get over the shock, even with a tenner in my pocket.

I bought a bunch of daffodils for Mother instead. I always bought daffodils for Mother in the Spring.

PLEASE REPORT

Night bombing was very heavy at this period and Dad, with other members of the Home Guard stood available every night of the week on a rota system. He used to be very tired if he had to be at the bank the next day. He was now almost 50 years of age. Brother and the Army Cadets were also expected to stand to their duties.

A very near miss for us hit the South Ealing Power Sub-Station and did a great deal of damage in that quarter. Three houses on the south side of Ealing Common just disappeared. Ealing Broadway's main shopping area was a mass of flames on one raid and a land mine just missed St Mary's Church. The docks were bombed nearly every night.

Our concert party was going from strength to strength and sometimes a 'big name artist' would appear with us at some of the 'Workers Play-time' shows. Our area took in some parts of Surrey, Middlesex and Berkshire.

Ken wrote to say he was near Blackpool, training to be a wireless operator air gunner. I am convinced that there was an awful lot of 'luck of the draw' as to which aircrew trade one got into, and the time of the application had something to do with it as well. Later on in the War, fully trained pilots were being used as 2nd Pilots in gliders. Certainly, in 1942 I would have been used as an air gunner if I had failed my pilots course. My navigation by chart was not that good and Bomber Command demanded the best available (rightly so, three hundred miles into Germany was no place to get lost).

May brought the shorter nights, which cut down the time over England for the German Bombers and our night fighters with new ASD equipment were obtaining more 'kills' for their efforts. Up until now, it had been a thankless task searching for raiders with the help of searchlights.

Early in the month I was told by the RAF to report for 'Assessment' at the Aircrew Selection Centre, Weston-Super-Mare, and I was forced to confess to my joining up. Barclays accepted the inevitable and I was given a day off which, joined to a Sunday, was sufficient. Saturday mornings were always worked in the banks and most offices, the only privilege allowed was that one could wear a sports jacket and flannels, ostensibly in order to go directly from work to the sports club. Sometimes I played a game of soccer for Barclays, but I had so many other interests I could not be a regular.

Upon arrival at Weston that day, I was told, together with a few hundred other hopefuls, to line up in threes in the station yard. Brought to attention and quick-marched, I was quite surprised at the co-ordination we managed. We marched for five minutes or so until we reached Weston's equivalent to the shore-end of a pier, a building usually reserved for ballroom dancing and cafeteria.

Upon arrival we were split into smaller units and allocated accommodation. In my case this was a small Bed and Breakfast Hotel where individual small kit was left. From then on we didn't stand still for two days. Educational tests, Medical tests, Aptitude and Endurance tests, every jolly test one can think of. All this, I gather, to decide which chap could do which air job best. I suppose there must have been some sense in it, but to me we all seemed equally fit and intelligent.

One test I was hopeless at and had to resort to cheating in order to even score. The task was to recognise coloured dotted numbers within a square of thousands of coloured dots. I am unable to recall the exact skulduggery I engaged in, but I had to resort to it several times in my RAF career as the test kept cropping up. The exercise was to test for colour blindness. The stupid thing is that I am not colour blind, but I do admit that a patterned roll of wallpaper stands an excellent chance of being alternately hung upside down.

When night fell, we were free to do as we pleased. I went to a dance but there were so many fellows and so few girls that it was a bit of a joke. The next day was similar to the former and we were released quite late to catch trains home and these embryo airmen came from every corner of Southern England. Travelling by train in wartime Britain was no fun. Most travellers were carrying heavy luggage, trains were in constant use because of the numbers being transported and little or no food was available. Some main stations were well served by the voluntary services, the ladies of which toiled away for hours dispensing tea and cake. The rationing system was beginning to bite hard and, although the serviceman was catered for, there was little food to spare.

When darkness fell, window blinds were tightly drawn and no interior light was allowed to escape, not that there was a lot of light inside the carriage as the bulb wattage was very low and about 50% were coloured blue. There were first class compartments but these were reserved for first class passengers only. All commissioned ranks travelled first class. To cap it all every traveller seemed dog tired and spent the journey draped over his or her neighbour. The corridors were almost impassable, filled with not too fresh smelling humanity (the whole atmosphere was wreathed in cigarette smoke) and one's feet constantly stumbled over kit bags and cases. Gas masks were another encumbrance, worn diagonally across the body, the rear of the wearer protruded six inches further than God made it, making it difficult for fellow passengers to pass.

Steam engines predominated in those days and the noise, smoke, steam and generated heat could become unbearable, but at the same time the experience was challenging and an air of excitement abounded. British Rail had not yet raised its head and each region of the country was served by its own line; London Midland and Scottish, London North Eastern, Great Western, Southern. All great railways and each very individual, and proud of their great locomotives. In such a manner we travelled home from our first contact with the RAF at Weston-Super-Mare.

From now I awaited each postal delivery anxiously. I usually left for the office before the post arrived and each day dragged before I could be off home to check the mail. Time seemed to stand still and I carried on my job without great enthusiasm. Not even Miss Gould's caustic remarks could spur me to any great efforts.

Greaves, the ledger clerk, was suddenly spirited off to the Army. Like me, I think he had been feeling the strain of waiting. Cake shops were still selling cakes and buns. The staff gave Greaves a farewell tea and cake party but nobody ever stopped working at their ledgers. Tea was always taken on the hoof.

Greaves' replacement arrived. 'She' was not what anyone expected, very painted and a bit scruffy with it. All right on top but I wouldn't have cared to look too deeply into the lady. One could tell that Arthur Jarvis was not impressed and he soon pushed me into doing far more of the ledger work while she did some of my tasks. She was about 25 years old and could be quite provocative, but I was very wary and made a point of never being in the office on my own with her. Miss Gould, bless her, sensed this and became all protective towards me, so I was never compromised.

London was packed with troops on leave and Piccadilly Circus became a famous meeting place. I suspect it always has been anyway, but just now Piccadilly Circus took on a new image. Eros was boarded up and the lights were dimmed, but somehow it was almost as though it was the very hub of the Universe. Not just England, not just part of a war game, but a symbol of the defiance of London against any enemy. The Londoners were defiant and they were certainly united. People cared very much about others, kind and thoughtful actions were seen everywhere. There was not a lot of mistrust and in Ealing where we lived, a door was seldom locked. Of course, there was always 'The Spiv' out to sell something which had fallen off the back of a lorry, and in Dockland half a meat carcass used to get 'lost'. By and large though, the populace did not approve of this sort of thing, and it became established that "a little fiddle was OK, but not a big one". That is human nature anyway.

May and early June passed before I heard a word from His Majesty, then a buff envelope arrived through the letter box. I was breathless as I opened it and read "Please report to RAF ACRC Lords Cricket Ground on July 14th 1941. Your rank will be Aircraftsman 2nd Class and training will commence from that date as Pilot U/T (Under Training)". Mother was silent, Father was pleased for me and Alan leapt about with me in sheer delight.

The next morning I proudly told each one of the staff individually and they all slapped me on the back in congratulations. Apart from Miss Gould that is, she just smiled and a few seconds later I saw her hastily drying an eye as she sat in her little cubicle before her typewriter. I got a cake and tea party too.

BISCUITS AND BILLETS

July 14th was a fine warm summer day and fluffy cumulus clouds scudded across the sky over central London. Unlike so many of my fellow trainees, it had been no great pain for me to leave home and arrive at Lords Cricket Ground, as it was an hour's journey at most. Some had to travel from Scotland overnight and from talking to those from miles away I realised they were feeling far from home. One lad living in Motherwell had never travelled further than Edinburgh. I had at least the advantage of being here a few times before, on happier days when Patsy Hendren was knocking up ninety-eight and Big Jim Smith was driving his 'sixes' into the stand.

This was the home of the Middlesex County Cricket Club. There must have been two thousand of us, but the organisation was very efficient and within hours we were allocated to flights of fifty billets in the modern flats in St John's Wood Road, bordering Regents Park. 'Biscuits' were dished out and three of these made a single mattress. Uniform came in pieces, but within three days we were kitted out. Not everything fitted perfectly, but at least we looked like airmen.

Eating arrangements left a lot to be desired as it could take one and a half hours from leaving the billet to arriving at the London Zoological Gardens Cafeteria to eat. The cafeteria was only a stone's throw away, but as we all left at the same time we were marched around Regents Park stopping and starting in our flights until our turn came. Upon arrival we were given twenty minutes to eat, before the order "7 Flight Fall In", caused the slow eaters, of which I was one, to ram any unfinished articles of food into our gas mask cases for later consumption. We had all been issued with knife, fork and spoon and after a quick dip of these into a running water sink, they were placed into the left-hand breast pocket where they remained until the next meal.

Drill became the most important thing in our lives and it was not long before my bank clerks' feet complained bitterly about stiff RAF boots. Several visits to the sick quarters were of no avail and apart from isolated days when I was 'excused boots' nobody cared very much. Obviously only army feet had to be nurtured, RAF aircrew would hardly need them.

The days were not without interest and the corporal in charge of the flight was forever shouting for us to 'fall in' or 'fall out' and the odd test was still being given.

We were worried about failing the night vision test, but none of us did. This was quite surprising in view of the fact that the whole operation took no more than five minutes from being outside the room in brilliant daylight, then inside in nearly total darkness, where certain shapes had to be identified, and then back into bright sunlight again. This was because a further one thousand nine hundred and fifty airmen were lined up in Regents Park awaiting their turn. For me, who always used to fall down at least one step in the local cinema if the programme had started, it seemed little different and I saw nothing from the time I went in until I came out.

Photographs, fire drills, guard duty and inoculations all took their turn. I was quite surprised to see so many tough fellows keel over in a faint as the needles went in. The word 'Aids' was not known and it was perhaps just as well.

Lined up with the others to get my jab, I was not the slightest bit concerned, but I do remember having to take deep breaths at an open window of a stairwell in order to regain my composure. Many people are affected in this way and I saw it happen again a year later.

Some evenings we were 'allowed out' and these few hours were heaven. I had a girlfriend who worked in Harrods and I used to meet her and have supper in Lyons Corner House, Marble Arch.

One afternoon I got along to Melbury Court and presented myself to be admired in my new uniform. Miss Gould thought I looked very nice and I was pleased. I was proud to be in uniform and wanted to do what I could to help the war effort.

The Prudential Assurance Co for which Betty worked had been evacuated to Southport. She took a weekend leave and as I had not seen her for several weeks it was nice to meet again at the YWCA dance.

My Mother asked me how I was liking service life and I told her it was all right but I was not keen on the swearing and bad language and the lack of bathing facilities was irksome. It used to be wonderful to get home and lie in the bath for an hour. Life had certainly changed in a fortnight. Air raids at night were a nuisance as we had to turn out to shelter in the lower floors of the flats but apart from a great deal of noise I never saw much damage done.

On the 28th July the Flight was confined to barracks all day. I was so bored out of my mind that I volunteered for a working party which turned out to be loading kit into railway wagons at Paddington Station. I got no thanks for working but at least it kept me sane. I arrived back in barracks at St John's Wood to be told I was 'Bloody Well Late', to get my kit and join the rest of 7 Flight in trucks waiting to take us to, guess where, Paddington Station. I didn't mind being 'beggared' about but I did object to missing my tea.

The journey was one of those I have already described. Starting at 11:15 from Paddington we headed West travelling through the night, which was usual with troop movements and the journey to Torquay took well over seven hours. It was wonderful to leave the stale smell of the train in the morning and form up in the station yard. Kitbag on shoulders and wearing greatcoat we were marched up to Babbacombe three miles to the East.

Here we found No. 1 Initial Training Wing and the larger hotels had been taken over by the RAF. Some hotel names come back to me; Sefton, Bay View, Trecarne, Babbacombe Bay. If we had to change squadrons, sometimes due to falling behind with progress, we changed hotels as well. I was always falling behind, so I knew nearly all the hotels in Babbacombe.

The sergeants in charge of the squadrons were a cheerful bunch, nearly all 'Come on, jump about' types and we were not surprised to find many quite famous sports personalities amongst them. At one time I was being bullied by Len Harvey, Middle Weight Boxing Champion of Great Britain. Freddie Mills, another boxer of repute, was also an instructor and there were many others as well. They were ideal chaps for the job, as being all very fit fellows ourselves, we looked up to them.

The officers were a different breed. All 'Wingless Wonders' Flying Officers and Flight Lieutenants, they were of a studious type with not a lot of humour.

The course was normally of eight weeks duration and in that time we were expected to become proficient at Foot Drill, Aircraft Recognition, Morse, Maths, Basic Navigation, Semaphore, Air Force Law, Armaments, and Administration. When we were not at this, fire piquet, guard duty or general scrubbing, we used to get down to the beach which was quite unspoiled and beautiful.

August was a fortunate time to be in sunny Devon and with all the exercise and swimming, I became very fit. The food on the whole was good but I used to look forward to parcels of fruit cake and goodies from Mother; a pair of knitted socks or jumper also used to arrive. I think that the whole of Queen Annes Gardens chipped in to help with the rationed items. Our neighbours were so very kind. I did not drink very much but after church parade on Sunday mornings I felt very Macho lifting a half pint of Mild and Bitter to my lips.

Pay was 32 shillings a week so I had a little more in my pocket than I had as a bank clerk but I was always hungry.

My ability to forget a subject when I feel I have finished with it is without parallel. It took the RAF just two weeks to find out that my maths, outside of basic arithmetic, was appalling. Algebra and Geometry were gone for ever in my brain but the RAF deemed them important. Progress exams were a constant embarrassment and at one interview with the CO he asked, "Berryman, when you were a bank clerk, which bank employed you?"

I proudly replied, "Barclays, Sir."

He turned to the Warrant Officer beside him and said, without a smile, "Remind me to nip down to Torquay tomorrow. I must change my bank account to Lloyds."

The work was a struggle for me as on top of poor Maths I found Morse difficult. Even at my best I could not receive more than six words a minute. I could send Morse much faster but the receiving was the important part.

September 1st arrived and with it my 19th birthday. The family, all praise to them, had rallied round to say I was not forgotten. It was a wonderful day. After church parade I had my usual half of beer and after lunch treated myself to a horse ride and a cream tea at a little village called Wattcombe, just along the cliff.

Saturday nights we all looked forward to. Ballroom dancing was the relaxation, Torquay Town Hall the venue. Numbers 3 and 5 ITW's were also in Torquay and many hundreds of us used to crowd into the ballroom. The orchestra was excellent, using saxophones and clarinets in the style of the 'Big Bands' of those days. It was unbearably hot and shirt order was allowed. Jackets off and tunic belt worn around trousers. Our shirts were very new and quite thick and stiff. The perspiration used to roll down our backs but we danced and laughed as if our very lives depended on it.

The girls were great. There were a lot of them and no airman was refused a dance. Of course, I fell in love. Muriel England was her name, she was nicknamed 'Cis'. I felt the love affair had gone on for ages but 45 years later I see by my diary it was in fact three weeks. Life was very vital and lived at a great pace. 'Cis' was a pretty girl with Monroe looks. We had fun together and I saw her as often as I was able, sometimes arriving late in Billets and having to do extra duty punishment as a result. She took me to her home and her parents were very hospitable. We loved very innocently but she went out of my life six months later when she died of Tuberculosis. I visited her family after the war and they were still heartbroken.

On October 1st, to our delight, flying kit was issued, much of which I carried about with me for years and never wore. However, I did not realise this at the time and it seemed a step in the right direction. Final examinations were taken hurriedly and we were told to take Embarkation Leave for two days.

Another night journey got me to London where the family were glad to see the prodigal son again. A London Palladium show Black Vanities was squeezed in somehow, a rush round relatives to say 'Cheerio for now', and I was back on the train to

Babbacombe. New tunics and caps were issued, kit bags were marked 'ARNOLD DRAFT', Leading Aircraftsman Propeller Badges were sewn on our tunics and with a fond farewell to 'Cis' I embarked on a train with many others. In the morning we arrived at Wilmslow, near Manchester, and the less said about that camp the better. Arrival date was October 11th and we left again on the 13th to arrive at Greenock, Scotland on a wet and windy morning, cold, depressed, tired and very hungry. Outlined against the Scottish hills bordering the Clyde, several large ships tossed uneasily at anchor and tenders were busily going about their business. It was a dramatic scene and I could not help but be overawed by it. One ship larger than the rest appeared to be receiving more attention than the others and we were told it was one of the fastest ships then on the ocean. It was the SS Louis Pasteur. Was this to take us on a journey of adventure we would never forget?

Two months to the day from standing in Lords Cricket Ground being given my forage cap with white flash (which denoted Aircrew Under Training) I found myself climbing a steep gangplank to the deck of the Pasteur and thought "Good Grief the Air Force must mean it. They are going to train me to be a pilot after all."

I knew my progress so far had been a series of near failures and it was most gratifying to feel that all was forgiven and I was on my way to my goal. Surely, I felt, they would not go to all this trouble for nothing. There had been the fear of elimination in all our minds and one or two hopefuls had already left to be trained for jobs other than aircrew or been sent for Wireless Operator Air Gunner training, in England. Here I was however, climbing a stairway to the stars and the time was 1:20pm on 14th October 1941.

PASTEURS NEW

Completed at St Nazaire in 1939, Pasteur's 32000 Tons were intended for the South American route but war came and she made her maiden voyage to Canada carrying French gold to keep it out of German hands. Cunard operated her as a troopship until she was handed back to the French Government in 1946 when she continued to serve as a troopship until 1957. For six war years the Germans tracked and hounded her with their U-Boat packs. They got her in the end though she was not sent to the bottom of the sea. She was to ride the waves in magnificence again as the North German Lloyd owned BREMEN.

It was soon learned that this voyage was to be once again to Canada (Halifax, Nova Scotia, in fact). With close on two thousand others I was to remain aboard for eleven days, nine of which were at sea on passage.

Because troopships of this size may never be used again, I shall attempt to describe the journey briefly.

Due to the numbers aboard, it was impossible to keep the ship very clean. The weather was wet the whole time and the troops (mostly Royal Navy and RAF) lived and slept in hammocks on mess decks below.

I recorded in my diary, "Wednesday, terrible crush, dirty and dull. Thursday, even more dirty and dull. Friday, first move at 09:30."

The next days read:

"Passing Hebrides, very rough, dozens seasick, feeling rotten, enemy bombers, action stations, escorted by two destroyers and one aircraft carrier." The destroyers, I remember, were old four-stackers, part of the US lease-lend agreement.

"Existing on bread and oranges." This was because I volunteered for work and found myself distributing fruit from the ship's cold store.

"Feeling better, found a decent place to sleep." This decent place was on the boat deck, hidden amongst the life preservers, quite illegal, but I could not stand the atmosphere below.

"Ran into a 78 mph gale, decks awash, everyone kept below deck, speed almost nil. Feeling better every day, ship moving very fast this morning. Escort has now left us, getting colder."

The ship's public address system called for helpers for the Ship's Concert. I went to the meeting and was introduced to an ordinary seaman who appeared to know what he was about. He was a tall good looking man and I was surprised at his cultured voice and confident air of authority. Together we rattled up a five-piece band and some good acts. I did my ukulele and impressionist act, while he made a fairly good job of singing "Mad Dogs and Englishmen Go Out in the Midday Sun". It was then I realised this ordinary seaman was Michael Redgrave, the celebrated actor. We did mix with some unusual people. In 1985 Sir Michael Redgrave still remembered this occasion in his book.

Whilst researching this information, by reading his book, it became obvious that he had recently been befriended by Noel Coward, and liked to be seen in the Noel image. That is perhaps why he chose to sing "Mad Dogs and Englishmen". In November 1942 Redgrave was discharged from the Navy and returned to the London Stage.

The first sight of Canada was on Saturday 25th October and I am not alone in my remembrance of the occasion, as I have since met two ex-airmen who were arriving that morning. We agreed that the shoreline looked bleak with thousands of coniferous trees rising up to the skyline. Within eight hours the ship had docked and my feet touched the Continent of America.

A train pulled by the huge American type locomotives brought the RAF contingent to Monkton, Nova Scotia, an excellent transit camp run by the Canadian Air Force. To young men from beleaguered Britain, the food offered was of gigantic proportions and we ate our fill. The lights in the towns, where no blackout prevailed were another joy and the Canadians were very hospitable.

Being a member of the YMCA was a help and opened a few doors for me. I soon got to know a few pleasant girls and was invited home. Some extra items of kit were issued, I learned about Halloween for the first time and suddenly I was on a train bound for Detroit and onward to Alabama with a bunch of chaps who were hitherto virtually unknown to me. Friends of three months were often split up and despatched to widely scattered flying schools.

My eyes were wide with amazement as I watched this strange countryside roll by as the train sped south, to arrive at the City of Montgomery, Alabama with a hiss of steam and the shouts of the coloured porters. I had not seen a lot of coloured people before and to see so many going about their everyday jobs was strange enough in itself.

Arrival at the US Army Air Corps base to the sounds of a full military band made something of an impression, as did the beautifully equipped quarters where we were to be housed. I read the multitude of orders and rules, surveyed the immaculate rifle I was issued with and sized the situation up profoundly by recording in my diary on November 7th, "There is a lot of bullshit here".

This last entry was an understatement. The US forces were on a peacetime basis and the standards were very high. To my eyes it seemed to be bordering on the ridiculous. Making one's bed with the corners squared off was acceptable but to measure the angle of the corner using a protractor seemed a bit much. To those of us who had already seen some of the ravages of war, the nit-picking seemed superfluous.

The training was carried out with, and in competition with, US Army Air Corps Cadets. Generally they were of much higher military standard than we British. They were larger in build, stronger, and better educated. On the sports field our teams had a job to keep up. They appeared to accept all discipline without question but one thing was lacking I thought – self discipline. They could be very childish. I reasoned that perhaps this was why the US Army imposed such pettifogging conditions on all of us and a lot of things we were expected to do were humiliating.

The British on the whole were very self disciplined and hardly required such rules. I cannot say I found my short service with the Air Corps to my liking and I was soon to learn the Air Corps felt the same about me.

Living conditions meanwhile were superb, the food magnificent, the camp servants pleasant and the people of Montgomery generous to a degree. The girls were beautiful and attentive. There was still no war in the USA. They could enjoy another month of peace.

None of us in the British Squadrons were very 'au fait' with rifle drill and the Armistice Day Parade on November 11th nearly produced our first casualty of the war when a little guy from Scotland took a chunk out of an Englishman with his fixed bayonet. This nearly provoked an international incident but a couple of days in hospital saw the injured party returned to us. In a nut shell, it was six weeks of parades, marching, brass bands, athletics, games, Guard Duties, fatigues, washing, cleaning, Arms Drill, Foot Drill and frustration. I just wanted to start my flying training, and I was not alone.

The war news was abysmal. In the Far East we had lost Malaya and Singapore. Two capital ships, HMS Repulse and HMS Prince of Wales, had been sunk by Japanese bombers. The Middle East and Mediterranean Theatre had seen British reverses and the British Army had retreated to Alamein. Letters from home were anything but encouraging and as if to cap everything the Japanese attacked Pearl Harbour and the USA was at war.

We cheered ourselves up when the base put on a very professional entertainment. Staged in a large hangar, with an audience of over two thousand, it was the best show I was ever to appear in, and the last, for a long long time.

PUT IT IN YOUR PIPE

On December 17th I boarded a train to Arcadia, Florida, US Air Base, where I was to start my flying training.

On the 18th I arrived at the Air Base and once again my diary shows admiration for the establishment but irritation with the discipline. Today I find this difficult to reconcile as I had had no problems on that score to date and my life style has always been very disciplined. I did not take kindly to the 'Hazing' system or the

'Honour' code. Hazing meant that any jumped-up twerp of a cadet, be he British or American, could order you to do the most stupid things. Hopping like a frog or flying like a chicken with appropriate sounds, were two Hazes I recall. One or two American cadets got away with it with me when I first arrived, but a Senior British cadet accidentally fell into the swimming pool later on. The Honour system meant that if one of your colleagues broke a rule, you were honour bound to report him for it.

If a cadet had flown solo he could wear his goggles on his forehead, if not, they were to dangle round the neck. Grapefruit at breakfast sometimes had to be eaten with goggles over the eyes. To me, at the time, it was a lot of damn nonsense.

Three days after arrival I flew in an aircraft for the first time and the normally enthusiastic 'me' confided to my diary "I cheered as I threw a leg into the cockpit, but the flight was not such a thrill after all."

Lord knows what I expected, a flight to the moon perhaps. Cape Canaveral was only an hour away, but I was 25 years too soon.

Between then and Christmas I nattered on about minor frustrations, then I got nabbed in the swimming pool when it was "Off Limits" (Out of Bounds) and I was awarded five days CC. Christmas Day came and went with an entry bound to make my family smile. "Xmas Day, and what a day, bored stiff, glad when its over to get some rest."

Some flying after Christmas must have placated me but by January 1st I write "HAPPY NEW YEAR – Like H—L. Spent last night in the town jail."

This never-to-be-forgotten few hours of my life occurred just after midnight in the town of Arcadia. I had not visited Arcadia before and I was surprised to find it resembled something straight out of a John Wayne film. Horses were tied to rails outside saloons and many premises had the stable doors which the hero always kicks aside to get in.

As I have explained, I was no drinker and this evening was no exception. I was not the least bit surprised however, to find a Scot by name of Jock Brodie, one of the British Cadets, sitting in the gutter singing "I Belong to Glasgow". A friend, John Cooke and I picked him up and hailed a taxi, which turned out to be a Police Car containing two officers. Out jumped the Sheriff complete with star on shirt, grabbed Brodie and started to bundle him into the back seat. Brodie resisted, so the Sheriff hit him with his night stick. That was too much for Cooke and me and we sailed in.

The jail house was situated on the edge of the town. It was a square box with a door and two grilled windows. Inside it had two compartments. One appeared to be full of rowdy drunks, the other contained two complaining prostitutes. Cooke and I were not rowdy but we were certainly complaining, so they shoved us in with the prostitutes.

Early the next morning, an American Lieutenant got us out. The charge read 'Resisting arrest and referring to the Sheriff as a Gouty Gorilla.'

The flying was going quite well and I liked my instructor by the name of Sessler. He was an unusual type for a US Air Corp Flying School. He was not an Army pilot and was as scruffy as you can imagine. He had a cheerful grin and smoked a lot of cigars, sometimes in the aircraft. I am sure he liked me and he told me that he had previously been employed by a flying circus and every now and again he would demonstrate some of his more spectacular stunts.

The aircraft we were using were PT17's, a biplane made by Stearman, a Company later to be incorporated with Boeing. They are super to fly and resembling a small Fairey Swordfish. I got on well with Sessler and went solo in six hours and forty minutes. Up to about 35 hours flying I was doing well, but approaching my fortieth hour check, I began to show signs of unease. Later to be a flying instructor myself, I now recognise the symptoms. Diary entries like "feeling tense, flying lousy, tight as a drum, got bawled out, feeling worried", start to appear. This continued until an Army 40 hour progress check, when a terse statement "Sessler's been sacked" appeared.

My new instructor, Poynter, had to suffer me for a further nine hours and twenty-five minutes, and I doubt if there could have been a lot of improvement, but the method of instruction was very different. I was then checked out by the senior army Captain. Terribly nervous, I did not give the chap a good ride. Safely on the ground he climbed out of the front seat, looked me straight in the eye and said, "Mister, you will kill yourself as sure as God made little apples. You are suspended." The ground could have swallowed me up and I would not have cared.

The next three days seemed like three years and I was told I had three days more to use as I wished. That morning I received a letter from Ian Garnham, one of the Ealing YMCA brigade. He wrote from Coral Gables University, Miami, where he was under training as an observer. I had little money, but a 'hitch' got me to Fort Myers, and a Greyhound Bus on to my destination. Arriving in Miami at Midnight, I slept at the least expensive hotel I could find and the following morning found Coral Gables and the University. I soon found Ian and told him my tale of woe. Being old buddies he quickly recognised that the money situation was not at its best and arranged for me to become an Observer Under Training for 36 hours.

During the day when they were working, I 'did' the town and beaches. When they ate and slept so did I. Unlike we pilots, the Observers were subjected to little or no military discipline, being treated like University students. There was no check on numbers, nobody noticed one more and so it was a cheap visit.

I was not very impressed with Miami and wrote, "Just mix Torquay with Blackpool and you have seen it all." From what I hear it is not all that different today.

The date was February 13th, a Friday, when I was in Miami and after arriving back at Arcadia I spent an unhappy day bidding my buddies farewell. For the record, and to emphasis the standard to which the US Air Corps were working, the six British students living in my billet had all been eliminated. I was the last to go.

I had seen some of Florida however and had visited Sarasota, Tampa, Fort Myer, Keywest, seen the Everglades and slummed it in Miami. One more formality had to be endured before I was returned to Canada as a rather unkindly worded 'Wash Out' and that was an 'Elimination Board'. This was a panel of RAF officers from Washington, sitting to soften the blow and redirect the unfortunates. It was then I had the good fortune to meet Arthur M Rees. Arthur also had been 'Washed Out', after 25 hours flying.

He was from a course after me (42G) and as we sat waiting to be called for interview I realised this man was nobody's fool. Aged 28, a big man with a small moustache, I later discovered he was a Cambridge University rugger blue, had visited Harvard and Yale Universities, was a Metropolitan policeman, played regularly for Glamorgan and had been capped for Wales. Arthur had a very Welsh voice and he was called in before me.

I could not help but hear the whole interview as I waited. He stormed and rated, banged the table and criticised the training methods unmercifully. He finished with "If you think I have come all this way to be told I can't fly an aeroplane after only 25 hours instruction, you are bloody well wrong! You can put that in your pipe and smoke it." I was to hear him use this phrase often.

The door opened and Arthur emerged. I was asked to enter. Two officers and a sergeant sat behind a desk in temporary stunned silence, looking embarrassed. I looked back, and realising I had to use the moment to its best advantage, cleared my throat and said in a firm voice, "And that goes for me too!"

Arthur and I were the first US trained failed pilots to be transferred to a British Flying Training School and within two days we were on a train to join a course at No. 1 BFTS Terrell, Texas, where we were allocated the same instructor. We became firm friends, and I am happy to say he survived the war as a Mustang pilot. He returned to the Police, retiring as Chief Constable of Staffordshire, where he was involved in the 'Yorkshire Ripper' case. His great love of rugger kept him on the Welsh Selection Board for many years and at the age of Seventy he managed the Crawshay XV Tour of South Africa in 1985-86.

From the moment I arrived at Terrell I felt really at home and from then on I cannot remember feeling the slightest worry about my flying ability. Terrell was situated in Kauffman County, forty miles East of Dallas in the big wide open spaces. The town was larger than Arcadia and the local people showed great friendliness towards us. Perhaps this was because we were exclusively British and far from home comforts, whereas in Arcadia we had been integrated with American cadets for whom they felt no responsibility.

The course which I joined was No. 7 which had arrived three weeks earlier. No. 3 was just leaving to return to England having begun their training in May 1941.

The barrack blocks, externally white boarded, were kept scrupulously clean by coloured janitors, and the messing and cafeteria were homely but spotless. The food was slightly more slanted to British tastes than at Arcadia and there were plenty of young ladies working within the complex which gave the camp a more informal look. The flying instructors were all civilian apart from the Commanding Officer, Wing Commander Hilton. Administration was handled by S/Ldr Beveridge and Flight Lieutenant Palmer. A couple of RAF Sergeants completed the RAF staff personnel. Nearly all the ground training was handled by American civilians.

WOODEN HORSES AND COLD WATER

Mr Pettett, a six foot, six inch lanky American, was to be my flying instructor. He had a dry sense of humour and was given to long periods of silence. This was unusual in flying instructors and wherever he was he constantly whittled away at a sliver of wood. Seeing this peculiarity for the first time I asked, "What are you carving, Sir?"

"A dick for a wooden horse," he replied.

With this man I relaxed and my flying showed it. We were still getting the odd 'Washout' for return to Canada, but this fear had left me. Two weeks after arrival however, I was in trouble again. Seven days CC for flying North of the rail road, a forbidden area. I was pleased to be enlightened. I had not read the flying orders properly and would not have recognised the rail road anyway.

Visits to Dallas at a weekend were great fun and we seldom had to take a bus to get there. Each weekend there would be many cars waiting for our release, each car driven by a pleasant American girl. These lassies were all pretty, trim, well educated and a joy to be with. No nonsense was offered and none given in return. Kissing and cuddling at an outdoor cinema, at weenie roasts and honky tonks was allowed. Any cadet requiring anything more made arrangements further from home.

Before I made a firm friend in Dallas I spent an evening feeling lonely and spending too much money. At midnight I was faced with taking a taxi back to camp or getting a room at an hotel. I had insufficient cash for both. Expecting that I could hitch a lift to camp the next day, I chose the Hotel Blue Bonnet for a nights rest. There was no receptionist on duty but a cheerful coloured porter showed me to a room and solicitously enquired if I required anything further. If he had known the state of my finances he would have known that breakfast Sunday morning was a doubt for a starter, let alone anything else.

I bathed and returned to my room, the bathroom being down the corridor. Upon turning the key in the lock, I found the cheerful porter beside me.

"You sure you OK boss?' he enquired.

"Sure," I said and hopped into bed.

Before I had said my prayers and put out the bedside light there was another tap at the door. Inexperienced at hotel living, I called, "Come In." She did. Pretty as a picture, a little blond slim girl clad in a negligee. She put me at ease immediately with a smile, sat on the bed, noticed my tunic and started to talk about England.

I always made a habit of carrying a toothbrush but I had nothing else with me and I felt a little embarrassed as I sat up, revealing my bare chest and shoulders. I had a rough idea what she could be about, but cared not to mention the subject in case I was wrong. Outwardly calm I was quaking within. Not for nothing had the RAF marched me down to the cinema back in Swiss Cottage, London, to be shown several horrific films on VD. Remembering Arthur Rees' words about Ladies of Leisure, short and to the point they were, "You may as well stick your John Thomas out of the window boyo."

I tightened the sheets around my thighs. Quite undeterred, she stayed and we talked well into the night. She told me she was a college girl from Austin, Texas, who had given birth to a child whilst at University. Her family had disowned her and she had taken up the 'profession' in Dallas, where her child was being cared for by a relative. I told her about my family and home life and we laughed. I also informed her she was on a 'Mission Impossible' and showed her my remaining 75 cents. She laughed even more and left the room. Seconds later she returned with five dollars which she put into my tunic pocket. Then like a big sister, she kissed me and bid me goodnight. The following week I sought her out and repaid the five dollars. I met her several times more, once taking her to a very pleasant supper in the Stoneleigh Hotel, a very upmarket hotel on top of which was broadcasting station, 'KSKY – The Station in the Sky'. I never dared risk the act but I was sorely tempted. Who said Eve was dead?

When in Terrell, rather than Dallas, I spent my free time church-going, riding horseback, visiting cinemas and ten pin bowling. I was still very naive and stuck very much to conventional pursuits. My flying settled down and I did some night flying. I was more than impressed by seeing brightly lit cities from above. It all seemed a fairyland to me.

The school saw a few crashes here and there, one PT18 landing on top of another was good for a laugh. Both aircraft were written off but nobody was killed.

The British Ambassador to the USA, Lord Halifax, made a visit accompanied by his wife. He was extraordinarily tall and she very charming. The unit, of course, had to parade in full regalia and I remember feeling proud to be British. Soon after he left, the end of the primary course was in sight and I was asked to organise a cabaret as part of the Easter celebrations.

I cobbled some sort of a show together, but regret to say that I recall no details whatsoever. It could not have been too bad, as the Administration Officer made a point of thanking and congratulating me on the effort. I took my final check ride on Primary Course, got a good grading and started packing a bag for a week's holiday.

The holiday break had been organised by Louis Gross, the flight's Progress Checker. He owned a very large estate car, and offered to do a tour of New Mexico with some of us. The chosen few were Arthur Rees, Bill Cooke, Billy Humphrey, Ian Campbell, Tony Fairhead and myself. We were all good friends and of the same 'ilk'. Our journey was to take us westwards through Dallas, Fort Worth, Abilene and Sweetwater.

In Sweetwater we stayed overnight in a Tourist Centre which had a Honky Tonk dance floor nearby. For economy four of us had taken a family room and we spruced up a bit for a night out. I met an attractive girl with whom I got on like a house on fire and by 11:00 pm we were doing a bit of kissing on the veranda.

By the time the others retired to bed at midnight we were at the heavy petting stage and when she left at 1:00 am, disappearing into the night never to be seen again, I was in a very uncomfortable and frustrated state. The last hour had been frequently interrupted by my coarse fellow travellers urging me to retire. Nice educated shouts like "For Christ's sake come to bed you bugger" had not exactly furthered my cause with the young lady and as I bid her farewell I realised that the pain in my groin was excruciating. I walked painfully into the room, filled the washbasin with cold water and deposited 'my tackle' in the chilled water with a sigh of relief. I did not live that occurrence down for a long time, but I had progressed a long way from East Wittering and a draughty spy hole.

The following day's journey took us on to Odessa, Red Bluff Dam and, as the evening sun disappeared beneath the horizon, Carlsbad came into view where 50 cents per head provided an evening meal. Once again we slept at a Motel, crowding as many as possible into a room to save expense.

Being the bank man of the party, the team looked to me for money guidance and I realised that when all available cash was counted we were going to be twenty dollars short of a safe return the next day. I found the Post Office and sent the following wire:

"To Manager, Barclays Bank, DCO New York – With RAF Training Dallas. Holiday. Need Twenty Dollars. Please Debit My Account Barclays Melbury Court Kensington London. Father Manager Barclays Chelsea. Please Send Money To Sante Fe Post Office. Berryman."

I assured my colleagues that the matter was in hand. After our party was regaled by the Mayor, Chief of Police and Journalists of Carlsbad, we sped onwards to Sante Fe.

Now well into Prairie land it was easy to imagine the covered wagons crossing the cactus ornamented waste back in the 1870s.

About half-way between Carlsbad and Sante Fe we passed through a real cowboy town, Roswell, and soon after came across two cowboys on their horses. They were very simple people and just existed with the cattle. Introductions were exchanged, and they were interested to meet Englishmen, probably the first they had ever met. One of them was Luigi Segura and he rode a fine white horse. Ian Campbell asked him if he could ride and it was agreed that Ian should mount the other horse, a good looking roan. We all recognised Ian to be a competent horseman.

Ian came of an Army family and his early years had been spent in India. His father was Major General J.A. Campbell DSO, 7th Armoured Division (for the information of those interested in Army history) and his mother was an authoress of some repute. He joined the RAF from Cambridge University. I have a photograph of Ian, hand raised in salutation to his friends, and with the click of the shutter the horse bolted. The prairie is a large expanse, and we were quite horrified to see Ian still astride the charging animal as it headed for the horizon. Luigi Segura set off in pursuit and two hours later they returned, Ian still mounted and looking not at all abashed, but we saw that his uniform trousers were in ribbons. He related the story that he had finally run against a barbed wired fence, which the horse dragged him along for yards before he re-gained control. His poor legs and backside were terribly lacerated, but the horse was unscathed.

Ian smiled through it all, even to having the stitches inserted without anaesthetic in the next township. He was a courageous man. I expect he died that way too when he was killed whilst trying to escape after his 111 Squadron Spitfire IX was shot down over Italy sixteen months later. I still retain his last letter to me from Italy in which he says, "I expect to be pooping at and being pooped at by the enemy, but instead I am a bit bored escorting bombers." This was immediately prior to Allied landings on the Italian mainland. I will always remember him with great affection.

Arriving in Sante Fe at almost 2:00 am is not the best time to arrive, but we found accommodation and were away again the next morning early to the beautiful village of Taos. Renowned in the art world, Taos was set high in the nearby snow-capped mountains and surrounded by Navaho Indian villages. We could buy no mementos as all available cash was needed for food, shelter and petrol, and we were 1000 miles from Dallas. The Rio Grande Gorge was very impressive as it carved its way through the volcanic rock to the sea. With its source high up in the Rockies, it seemed strange to hurl stones across its width, as towards the end of the 2200 mile journey it becomes a massive estuary.

Towards the end of the day, I rushed to Sante Fe Post Office and yes the required cash had arrived, only my signature was required. With the money came a telegram, "Owing To Currency Regulations, Unable To Debit Your Account. Please Accept My Personal Loan. Good Luck Manager Barclays New York."

Words could never be said that would convey our joint thanks to that trusting and generous man. He was of course fully repaid eventually, but continued to send gift parcels to me until I returned to England. I know my Father wrote from London and thanked him, Bank Manager to Bank Manager, that was how banking was. Now I deplore the lack of personal interest shown by the Banks. With money in our pockets we could retrace our steps through Carlsbad towards Dallas. In Carlsbad, we collected newspapers containing a report on our visit, headlined "Our

Gallant British Allies." We saw a display of excellent steer roping, visited the town jail (which revived some unpleasant memories) and continued the last 500 miles home in one hop. The chaps would not stop in Sweetwater, as they considered Dallas a better bet for a full night's sleep.

Arriving in Dallas early on Sunday, completely without cash once again, I visited my friend at the Blue Bonnet Hotel who coughed up two dollars without me having to promise anything further than repayment.

We ate breakfast that day at 5:00 pm and slid into our RAF bunks near midnight. What a story we could write home about, but meanwhile the Basic Course commenced the next morning, Monday 4th May.

BACK TO BASICS

The Basic Course Training Aircraft, the BT13A, was a 450HP engined, fixed undercarriage, low wing monoplane. Larger and heavier than the PT17 it was a bit more of a handful, but it was comfortable and the perspex cockpit canopy kept some of the noise out. I was allocated to another instructor, Harold Rogers, and I liked him immediately. He was a good-looking bronzed Texan with a ready smile (and still had when we met again in 1986).

For the first time I admitted to being thrilled by flight, possibly because we started to be instructed in some of the more spectacular aerobatics, which was to me the best part of the training. Sessler had awoken the 'free bird' within me back in the Air Corps days, and when flying the BT solo and when I thought I was unobserved, I used to practice my steep turns in a vertical rather than a horizontal plane. After all, broadly speaking, a loop is just a steep turn done the other way. This attitude did not help other aspects of my flying and my diary is one long groan about having to sit under a hood flying by instruments.

From the start to finish of my training I was never congratulated on my instrument flying and progressed from test to test more by luck than judgement. I did not recognise the fact that I was developing in to a 'seat of the pants' pilot, a type not greatly appreciated in Bomber Command and something I had to correct myself in later years.

Flying in Texas was wonderful, weather conditions and visibility are as good as you can find. The towns stood out on the flat prairies like a sore thumb and every field was a potential landing ground if lost. The tales of pupils landing to ask the locals the way home are numerous, but that type of escapade never went unpunished if discovered. One chap, Colin (Tyler) Coulson got lost several times in the same area and for a week he was made to wear a cardboard backed map around his neck like a placard. Some of us smelt a rat when it happened once again, and it was discovered Tyler had a girlfriend living in his 'lost' area. He pleaded innocence to the charge of course and got away with it. We all considered him very lucky.

Over-confidence in young pilots is very dangerous and a hundred hours experience can produce just this. It was proved, tragically, to 7 Course when a young Scot from Dundee, Jock Craig, did some unauthorised low flying at nearby Wills Point, hit a radio beacon mast and crashed in flames. Two other pilots were with him, Ginger Kelly and Bill Cooke, who had been on the Sante Fe trip with me. Kelly and Cooke were immediately suspended and returned to Canada. Jock Craig was buried in Terrell Cemetery on May 29th. One of many, his grave is still cared for by the ladies of the town, one of whom I met at a BFTS reunion in 1986. The whole course was then punished with 14 days CC and 1 hour drill each evening.

Both Kelly and Cooke, top and bottom bunk mates, had recently bought gold watches from the local jeweller on a regular repayment system. Being unable to continue payments, another trainee and I undertook to keep the watches and to continue payment. Both Bulova wrist watches are still being used in my family today, a credit to Bulova as they have had a hard life but still continue to tick. The story of the watches I shall relate in turn.

Meanwhile if Bulova would care to donate a new watch in view of this advertisement I would be grateful.

Since the start of the Basic Course a lady had come into my life, of whom I was becoming very fond. Her name was Clarine Compton, daughter of a Dallas advocate and living with her family at 4900 Lakeside Drive, Dallas. We met by chance when I was with Arthur Rees one weekend and I think it was Arthur who first attracted her eye. She was older than I by a couple of years, had suffered an unfortunate marriage and was divorced. Her parents were wealthy people, their home being in the nicest area of Dallas. Father was an ardent prohibitionist, Mother an attractive socialite. Clair could drink most of us under the table, but that did not take a lot in those days. We always drank canned beer, 'Schlitz' being her favourite brew. Arthur and I were always welcome in the Compton household where we had our own suite of rooms.

Clair and I developed a pleasant friendship as I was a reasonably good dancer and she liked to dance in the better 'nite spots'. Meanwhile, I was being introduced to a way of life hitherto unknown to me. Arthur was my guide and mentor and before long I could weather all night swimming pool parties like a veteran (albeit a tired veteran). The weather was very hot indeed and as much time as possible was spent in and around swimming pools, and all Clair's friends had one. I hardly needed money, as she always paid if I couldn't, and her car was at my disposal at weekends.

The weeks flashed by and with all my night flying and cross country trips completed, I was due for a basic course check ride. My log book records that Van Lloyd, the Chief Flying Instructor, was to be my check pilot. During the check flight, Van Lloyd took me through a thorough workout and as we returned to the field he asked me to carry out a slow roll to the right. I had a quick gander round to see my air space was clear, put some throttle on and gently pulled the nose above the horizon and co-ordinated stick and rudder for the first part of the roll. With the aircraft on its back, with rudders centralised and stick forward, I applied top rudder to complete the roll, only to find that the rudders were locked solid. The resultant manoeuvre, completed entirely by aileron, took up a lot of sky, and Van Lloyd was decidedly displeased. It took a few moments to quieten his tirade, but I finally convinced him that the rudder bar was solid. Van wasted no time in taking over control, informing me that he was going to try and put the plane down on nearby Tarver airfield. Over the radio telephone I asked him what the chances of a safe arrival were. "Pretty good," he replied. "You can go over the side if you want." I looked at the ground 4000 feet below and decided it looked quite unyielding. I thought of my parachute packer whom I did not know, and I thought about Van whom I did.

"I am staying," I muttered.

"What?" said Van.

"Staying," I shouted. "It's all yours," and I raised both my arms above shoulder height to signify that if he was not flying the BT, nobody was. Despite being a gusty day he made a beautiful approach and landing. My faith had been rewarded.

"Not bad," said Van Lloyd as he walked away.

With that 'ride' I was due for a week's leave and Arthur Rees, Tom Ashworth, Harry Critchley, Tony Fairhead and I decided Galveston on the Gulf of Mexico was the place to go. Ian Campbell and Billy Humphrey said they were going in search of culture, as befitted their education.

Letters from home kept me in touch with a worsening war situation. I should imagine that if one had to evaluate the lowest ebb for the Allies it was probably now. In 1953 Winston Churchill was asked by Lord Moran, his doctor, to pick out the two most anxious months of the war. Winston replied September and October 1942.

In Europe – With the Germans in occupation the position was stalemate and their land forces were containing the Russians.

In North Africa – Tobruk had fallen, and the British Army had retreated to Alamein, almost to the Canal Zone.

In Asia – The Japanese had overrun in succession Malaya, Hong Kong, Borneo, Java, Sumatra and Burma. Their armies stood at the gateway of India.

The Air War – Over Germany, RAF Bomber Command had started their first 1000 bomber raids which was at least good for public morale. In other theatres the policy of constant pressure was maintained.

The Sea War – U-Boat Wolf Packs were harassing Allied shipping and our Merchant shipping. Losses were great, with 109 ships lost in May.

For 7 Course there was nothing we could do but go on leave and the five of us set forth to Galveston. We were fortunate with the weather and for three days we soaked up the sea and sunshine. On the Wednesday, however, the peace was shattered when Clair and her friend DA arrived from Dallas. We were staying at the inexpensive Beach Hotel, but the girls booked into the Galvez which was a bit more upmarket. This suited us very well as we more or less used the Galvez as the 'Club'. Late nights and sorry mornings became the pattern for another four days, when we returned relaxed and ready to surmount the final hurdle. Five weeks of concentrated advanced flying, covering eighty-five hours in the air lay before us.

The AT6A, or Harvard as it was better known, was the chosen aircraft and I fell in love with the aeroplane from the start. With a larger engine than the BT and a retractable undercarriage, it was a magnificent machine to throw about the sky, and with one hundred and fifty hours in my log book I did just that.

Each hour of experience was now bringing me closer to my goal, which was to fly Hurricanes or Spitfires. The chance to do this would be slim I knew, as Bomber Command made most demands for new pilots. The bomber offensive was being stepped up and replacements were needed for lost crews. I wrote in my diary on June 21st, "The end of a peaceful leave, I feel on the ball again. ATs here I come, I have dreamed of this day, but with any luck there will be a greater day to come."

Up until this time I treated my flying as a day to day experience. I had never in my life excelled in very much, but now it looked as though with luck and perseverance I could gain those coveted wings.

No. 6 Course had gone and I had watched their Wings Parade with envy, hardly daring to think it would one day happen to me. I am sure I became obsessed and nightly I prayed to God to let me die rather than fail.

The night flying became more demanding, the cross country flights longer, the Check Flights by Chief Instructors would really start the adrenalin running and ground school subjects became harder. Many evenings were spent studying or making up flight plans for the following day.

The diary entry for the 29th of the month records: "Terrible day, flying 7:00-12:30. Ground School 2:00-5:00. Exam 6:00-9:30 now 2 flight plans to complete for tomorrow." Nevertheless I still had time to play and I had fallen a little in love with Clair, so Saturdays and Sundays we danced, swam and laughed.

One evening at a night club I met my Flight Commander Charlie Orr, who was most amused when I won the 'Best Legs' Competition. I shared the Champagne prize with him. He liked Clair and our usual gang were in a rare mood. This occurrence was probably a bit of luck, as from then on he would after a formal greeting, refer to me as Nick. I felt that when we flew together, I was not just another cadet in a flying helmet. Certainly I never gave him a bad check ride, and his encouraging remarks added to my growing confidence.

On July 14th I remembered I had spent one whole year in uniform. It had to be a day to be remembered and it was. Despite my year of service, I had left no great mark to single me out as 'brilliant'. In fact Rogers, my instructor, often remarked to the contrary.

I was dispatched to Shreveport on a solo cross-country flight and upon finding the airfield, called on radio for permission to land. When I received the OK I started a circuit, only to find my undercarriage would not lower. I had a slight panic, feeling sure I must have forgotten to operate something, but no, the gear would not come unstuck. The Duty Officer at Shreveport told me to jigger off back to Terrell, as they did not want to cope with any mess I might make. When I arrived at Terrell the Control Tower could not believe my tale of woe, and told me to orbit the airfield at 3000 feet. Van Lloyd the CFI, who was beginning to associate me with disaster I am sure, came up on the RT and we chatted about the problem. I climbed to 5000 feet, put the aircraft into a very steep dive and pulled out hard with a lot of 'G', at the same time selecting 'Undercarriage Down'. This availed nothing, so with a wonderful excuse to show off, I tried selecting 'Down' at every conceivable flying attitude. Van Lloyd got the message, and told me to drop the aircraft down nice and soft alongside the landing directional T.

On the final approach I selected 'Undercarriage Down' again, as force of habit. I distinctly remember hoping they would not lower, as I had always wanted to try this and who would believe my story anyway. No. 1 BFTS had got word that there could be a bit of sport in the offing and a sea of faces gazed skyward. The watchers were probably disappointed as the aircraft touched down in a cloud of dust and with a lot of noise as bits fell off, it stopped. Within seconds there was a head alongside mine in the cockpit, checking fuel and switches were off. The Wing Commander was there as well.

"Come on out," he said, not sounding over-sympathetic.

I started to stand in order to climb out, and found to my embarrassment that I had no strength whatsoever in my legs. This was no time to prove to the World that I was just a chicken at heart, so I sat down again on my parachute. Pulling out the flight report from its pocket and with the dust still rising, I inserted the date and time adding the words, 'Duty carried out, undercarriage did not lower for landing.' The Wing Commander looked on in amazement, but what he did not know and I did, was that this was not a show of bravado, but a matter of sheer necessity.

The following morning I was flying again. This time it was to be a formation flight with Arthur Rees and Taffy Davis. I was to lead and we did a formation take off, the first I had ever done. We were at 1500 feet and still climbing when out of the corner of my right eye I spotted Taffy dropping behind with a faulty engine. I hardly had time to call him on the RT before he had pushed his nose well down to retain airspeed. I heard the words "B191 engine quit" and he was already headed for a likely looking ploughed field. I followed him down and saw him drop his flaps. He seemed more or less into wind and set to emulate my example of the previous evening. To my horror I saw a last minute change of mind and direction. He had decided to ignore the wind and land along, rather than across the furrows. He had left it too late and his port wing touched the ground.

Arthur, slightly above me, was already on the radio asking for help. Police training I suppose. Taffy's machine bounced once and cart-wheeled across the field, ending in smoking wreckage. The cockpit area was visible and I thought I saw him moving. There were some vehicles moving in his direction from the road. Arthur and I stayed for some minutes more, then Control ordered our return. A couple of anxious hours later, we heard Taffy was alive. When we saw him next, looking a bit superficially damaged, he made us smile as he related his moment of regaining consciousness.

He awoke on the counter of a small village drug store, laid flat, as a small boy leaned over his recumbent body proffering a nickel for a large ice cream cone. He recovered to fly again nine days later, once again in formation with me. My diary reads, "Taffy flying again, flew formation with him. Very uncomfortable ride. Had a feeling that if anything went wrong he would swing his ship into me. But he flew a nice formation, I must be scary!"

There was no time for relaxation, as the Wings exam was upon us. Navigation followed by Signals, Armaments, and Airmanship gave me cause to regret my inattention to my instructors, and I took a final flying check with Charlie Orr. The exam papers were assessed in Washington and a week of sick anxiety followed before I heard that I had passed all but the Engines subject in Airmanship. I was not alone, as nineteen others had failed something, but we could do a retake in one subject. I flew one more 'check' with the Wing Commander this time. I was a bit nervous and did a bad precautionary landing. Hilton was not given to displays of emotion and sat impassively as I put him through my aerobatics. We landed, he climbed out and for the first time I saw him smile. Every movement he made, appeared in slow motion to me. He removed his helmet and parachute harness before saying a word. When he did, it was not much.

"Rotten precautionary landing," he said, "but the aerobatics were as good as I have ever been given! By the way you passed your engines exam this morning, and I'm giving you an Above Average grade."

My heart nearly stopped and I felt close to tears. I looked skyward in relief – I am sure I saw old Sessler doing a couple of Upward Charlies.

In every military establishment there has to be a reward for excellence, and twenty-four pilots of 7 Course were to receive their wings before the nineteen first-time failures. We watched as they received their wings and marched to the railway station, whilst we had the distinct advantage of having sufficient time left to say farewell to friends. For me, this was to thank Clair and her family for their generosity. Clair's father asked me what I thought of things generally, and I replied, rather wittily I thought, "Jolly exciting, in view of the fact, that for me, the war has not yet started." Clair kissed me and we both promised undying allegiance. We have never seen each other since.

The next day we received our wings and left Terrell, bound for Canada. Only one thing marred the occasion. My good friend Harry Critchley had failed his Navigation exam for the second time and was not then awarded his wings. I felt very sad for him and refused to sew my wings or Sergeant Stripes on my tunic before we left Terrell. He did not stick out like a sore thumb; there were two wingless wonders waving farewell.

Taffy Davis completed his course by staying a further three weeks and Harry Critchley re-sat a wings exam at Trenton, Canada. He passed and spent quite a few months ferrying Mitchells across the Atlantic where he could not afford to make a mistake with his Navigation. Tom Ashworth passed out top of the course and was retained in Canada as an instructor for a year, before joining 249 Squadron in Italy, collecting a DFC, flying Mustangs and became their last wartime CO. Arthur Rees also became a Mustang pilot.

Billy Humphrey flew twin-engined aircraft and collected a double DFC on Mosquitos. Billy was a Lincoln City man and I later met his family. His brother, Andrew, became Chief of Defence Staff. Ian Campbell met his death after being shot down in Italy, and another twenty-two loyal chaps from 7 Course met theirs in the war-torn skies. Many of the students, particularly those from the early BFTS courses were awarded decorations and Arthur Aaron from 6 Course received the posthumous award of the Victoria Cross.

I was still 19 years of age and had not yet realised that to have been associated with men of this calibre was to be the greatest privilege of my life. Perhaps too, my family will not always smile when I refer to myself as a humble man.

The two and a half day journey to Moncton seemed long and dirty, but after taking leave of Harry Critchley in Toronto, I chatted up a French Canadian girl who sewed my wings and stripes to my tunic, in order that I was properly dressed upon arrival at the transit camp. For five days I kicked my heels impatiently and on the sixth day I boarded the RMS Strathmore at Halifax for the ten day crossing to Glasgow.

The journey could have been disastrous and our war over, for in the first 24 hours a German U-Boat attacked and sunk a tanker in convoy immediately astern.

TO JUMP OR NOT TO JUMP

My 20th birthday, September 1st, found me treading my native soil again. I was pleasantly surprised that the standard of living was still quite reasonable as I had gathered from letters that there were great food shortages. There were of course, but the Forces were somewhat protected.

Arriving in Bournemouth the following day, I lost little time in visiting Barclays Bank for some cash and telephoning my Mother, who was overjoyed to hear my voice again.

The next week saw me purchasing a commissioned officer's uniform from Moss Bros, playing cricket for Bournemouth Cricket Club and reporting sick with scabies, which I had collected on the boat. Ask anyone who has ever suffered the infection where the itch attacks mostly, and you will not be surprised to learn that a washbasin in the Royal Bath Hotel was one night similarly honoured in the same way as the washbasin in Sweetwater, USA (just the right height you see). Very hot baths and rough scrubbing brushes wielded by fearsome male nurses got me sorted out to enable me to take leave on the 8th September.

I arrived back in the family home, 10 Queen Annes Gardens, Ealing at 10:15 that night. I had told nobody of my intended arrival and arrived by taxi. The house was in darkness, but my knocking on the front door produced a light in the front bedroom above. A minute elapsed, the door opened and in the darkened hallway I saw my Mother, in her dressing gown and with her long hair hanging in a plait. She extended her arms and we embraced. She whispered "My Lamb! My Lamb!"

Father and Alan were soon on the scene and there was laughter and tears. It seems we were always doing one or the other for those years. Six wonderful days of leave and relaxation followed. Visits to relatives and friends, and tickets for my old favourite variety show at the London Palladium had me humming and tapping my feet to the latest songs. The glorious Tiller Girls, whose long slender rhythmic legs kicking away in perfect unison completed my happiness to be in England again.

A flying visit to see Betty, now nursing with the VAD at Woking Emergency Hospital, and I was again sitting in the Royal Bath Hotel, this time ordering a whisky and soda (the first I had purchased in my life). The RB was being used as a transit officers mess and when approached by a mess waiter asking what my evening beverage should be, I was so taken aback at being addressed as 'Sir', I thought half of beer might offend him.

More interviews with senior officers here must have decided my future RAF employment. They seemed to know quite a lot about everybody and had personal documents to refer to. I was shortly posted to 17 AFU Watton Norfolk and it was now that three other chaps entered my life. Charles Lawrence, Ray McNair-Taylor and Paul Mercer. We had all trained on the same course at Terrell, but had spent no time in each other's company, other than passing pleasantries as we handed over cockpit or lavatory seats. Now, segregated by the commissioned and non-commissioned officer status and single or multi-engined training, we were thrown together and moved to Norfolk. The journey took us through Norwich where I spent a happy day seeing Uncle Ernie, his wife Aunt Maude and a brand new cousin, Brenda, whom I described as 'very cute'.

AFUs (Advanced Flying Units) were an important part of overseas trained pilot progression, as many of us had never seen England from above before and the tightly-condensed towns and small fields could be confusing. The weather was quite different and low cloud was a new nightmare. Add all that to the fact that often four airfields were visible at the same time, and wondering which you had departed from, it is not too difficult to see the necessity to familiarise us.

At Watton I was an immediate success. Entrusted with a Miles Master aircraft, I set about orientating myself to the new surroundings. I flew Master aircraft for only twenty-one hours and in that time broke off two tail wheel assemblies, set fire to a third aircraft and totally destroyed a fourth. I did not like the Master and was delighted to be asked to travel North to Carlisle, where the RAF would be pleased to put a few Hurricanes at my disposal.

Together with my new found friends (Charles, Ray and Paul) I arrived at 55 OTU Annan situated on the Northern Banks of the Solway Firth (miles from Carlisle!). A mood of urgency prevailed here, as all the staff officers were tour-expired fighter squadron pilots who knew by experience that whatever was not learned now could lead to personal disaster. Upon leaving OTU the next stop was an operational squadron where Squadron Commanders had little time to spare for idiots.

I was introduced to a Hurricane on October 15th. The 16th was a red-letter day, a day I had dreamed of for a whole year. My sense of humour had not deserted me in this time and my log book and diary records Friday 16th October.

"Twenty minutes for a cockpit check, which I carried out about five times. Eventually ready to go – got off OK. Unable to find undercart lever. Terrible moments expecting to spin in any moment. Aircraft bucking about all over the bloody place. Climbed to 1000 feet, then selecting wheels down found myself at 1700 feet. Forgot radio procedure completely and forgot my radio call sign – suddenly cross wind turning to land, all became calm and she came in as gently and as easily as a bird – now at long last a Hurricane has flown me."

Not exactly a macho way of describing one's first flight in a fighter aircraft, but that is how it was and that is what I wrote. Over a beer in the bar that night I probably said "Hurricanes? Piece of Cake!"

The OTU Course was anything but a piece of cake in fact, as from now on it was all up to the individual. This was university after schooling. Advice we could get from instructors and flight commanders, but we ourselves had to learn to fly, fight and survive battle in the air. As a pure fighter, the Hurricane was being phased out in the European Theatre of War, its role being taken over by the Supermarine Spitfire V's and IX's and the Hawker Typhoon. The Hurricane was still an excellent fighter, having the decided advantage of being very manoeuvrable. Ten weeks of concentrated air fighting, gunnery and camera gun exercises were to begin. A typical day would take in formation flying, air-to-air firing using a towed drogue and experience in cloud flying. On the latter exercise, I realised I had to wake up or be shot up.

Instrument flying with the secure knowledge that there is a safety pilot in the back seat of a trainer is a bit different from leading a section of three single seaters up through the overcast to the sunlit expanse of sky above. This expanse was a wonderful playground where we learned our trade.

On the morning of November 1st I decided to do a bit of cloud flying, taking a look at Glasgow and Edinburgh while I was at it. When in the vicinity of Glasgow, I noticed a very rapid deterioration in the weather. I decided to forego the pleasure of viewing the smoky city from 6000 feet and turned on to a reciprocal course for base.

Feeling thoroughly relaxed I rolled a couple of times left and right, dived to the top of the clouds and pulled up into a loop rolling off the top. I was quite used to checking all the instruments for acceptable readings and was surprised to see engine oil and coolant temperatures rising.

Not worrying overmuch, I took off a couple of hundred RPM by reducing throttle and expected to see a reduction in temperature. I then noticed the engine was beginning to run less smoothly and a strong smell of glycol coolant was in the cockpit.

Knowing that I was over mountainous country and I was twenty-five minutes flying time from base, I decided not to find my way home by any other method than the fastest. I radioed for a course to base but received no reply. I persevered for a while longer, switched frequency and asked for assistance from anyone hearing me, but still no reply. The engine temperature was way above danger level now and the rolling clouds were immediately below me. I knew I had to stay on course and get through them safely. I had reduced the engine revs to little more than a tick over and I dropped fifteen degrees of flap to reduce to a safer angle and speed of descent. Now in cloud and with my eyes glued to the instruments, the glycol steam was wreathed about me. I slid back the hood and the fresh air rushed noisily in. Surely I would break cloud base shortly.

Knowing that the mountains thirty miles north of the Solway were reaching up to 2000 feet, I was a bit shattered to see the altimeter reading 3000. "Sod this," I thought, "I am for out." I slid the cockpit cover fully back, pulled the 'D' pin on the Sutton safety harness and knocked the ignition switches to off. Then grasping the top of the windscreen I started to pull myself up and into a standing position. The aircraft gave a lurch as I released the control column and instinctively I sat down again to centralise the swinging instruments, for what reason I shall never know. By the time stability was regained I was ready to go over the side, but noticed that the altimeter was reading just over 2000 feet, and unwinding fast. I realised I had left it too late to bale out.

My mind became crystal clear and knowing that I could be only 30 feet above a cloud-engulfed mountain peak, decided to stay where I was. One of two things would happen. Either I should reach cloud base and a chance to survive, or my life would be snuffed out like a candle. I had no last-minute thoughts, my whole life did not flash through my brain, I had no regrets, no thoughts of family, no fear of death. I stared fixedly ahead at my instruments, keeping my airspeed to a safe 120 mph.

I thought I saw a sudden change in the cloud colour and then in a split second I could see the ground. A feeling of relief surged over me, I knew I would make it now, but I had not a lot of time. A glance at the altimeter showed 900 feet and I saw a road and a farmhouse. "Anywhere there," I thought, "must be people to help if I turn over upon hitting the ground." Ahead I saw a collection of small fields some with livestock in them. Selecting the largest grass field, I pushed the nose down towards it, at the same time selecting full flap. The undercarriage could stay where it was, tucked away.

At 50 feet I passed over a low stone wall with my speed at about 85 mph and I wished it had been 10 mph slower. I was clearly going to run out of field before I could stall in, but I had no choice. Ahead was a huge mound of earth and stone stretching yards to left and right. I did not fancy ploughing into that and eased the old Hurricane's nose forward towards terra firma. Then she hit, and so did I. With all the uncertainty of baling out, I had forgotten to refasten the safety straps and my face crashed forward into the gun sight. With its large radiator under the fuselage acting as a scoop, the Hurricane stopped in only a few feet. I was spitting broken flesh and blood as I disconnected the radio and oxygen leads before climbing out. Then remembering I had not switched off the fuel, climbed in again.

Women and children were running from the farmhouse no more than 100 yards away and I knew I had survived. Within a few minutes I was seated in a warm farmhouse kitchen, feeling my face and asking for a mirror. To my relief I looked better than I had expected and gratefully accepted a cup of tea. An Army Sergeant appeared and told me that he had placed a guard upon the aircraft. He then made a phone call to the nearest RAF station which was Crosby on Eden some twelve miles away.

The farm family were very attentive and by the time the ambulance and crash crew arrived I was somewhat cleaned up. Enquiries as to my whereabouts revealed that I was at Gilsland, near Haltwhistle, and only twenty-five miles east of Annan. I had nearly got back.

As I was climbing into the ambulance, all the ladies there gathered, young and old, came forward to kiss my bloody face. They made it quite obvious they were grateful to Britain's airmen.

I glanced back at P2993 ZX-C looking reasonably undamaged in the middle of the field. "By the way," I said, "what is that ruddy great mound I landed just short of?"

"Oh, you would not have moved that," came the reply. "That is Hadrian's Wall."

2993 was repaired, sent to the Middle East and served with the Free French Air Force until struck from Air Ministry charge 28th August 1944. So she eventually followed me to North Africa on a later posting.

The ambulance sped southwards and arrived at a hospital in Blackpool, where the doctors sorted my face into a reasonable shape by sticking the top inside of my mouth to the lower inside of my nose which is where it belonged. The most hurtful part of the operation was being told not to eat solids for four days. Bodily, I was fit and hungry. My mouth was bruised, but not all that painful. However I was trapped, as there were too many nurses to see that I did as I was told. I rang home and told the family where I was and on the third day of bored confinement, a dark handsome RAF Sergeant stood grinning at me from the foot of the bed. I just could not believe my eyes, there stood cousin Ken.

Word had passed around the family that I was in Blackpool and Ken was doing an Armourer's course at Kirby, just up the road. Ken was very amused that this time it was I who was in trouble, and I had to agree it was a change.

He always had a winning way with him and together we conned Matron into letting me out for a 'gentle walk' for the afternoon. I had only flying kit to wear, but I managed to borrow a forage cap and with trouser bottoms pulled over flying boot tops I could pass muster. Together again and happy to be so, we were soon at a dance in the Tower Ballroom. Eating for me was not on, but nobody had mentioned drink.

A quick committee meeting decided that a few beers were in order and the Sergeant was in charge. He had to be, as only he had any money. With our thirsts slaked, we decided some female company would be appreciated.

Ken said, "You stay here, one look at your face will ruin both our chances," and went in search of two suitable ladies. The ploy worked and he returned with two friendly girls. The good-looking one was for him, and the other would be company for his 'war-damaged hero cousin'. Reginald Dixon, the resident Tower Organist, bashed away at all the popular tunes as we danced the evening away.

I was overdue at the hospital when Ken put me on a bus and paid my fare before hurrying off to his own base. The bus had an elderly driver and a lady conductor, and the engine refused to start up to commence the journey. Always helpful, I left my seat on the top deck and joined the puffing driver at the 'business' end.

The old chap was visibly distressed by his efforts with the large starting handle.

I offered to swing the handle whilst he operated the throttle. A couple of my enthusiastic swings started the bus at the cost of blood from my freshly doctored mouth. Unabashed, I alighted at the hospital entrance and reported to my ward where I was met by an irate night sister.

"Open your mouth," she said. I complied rather sheepishly. "You will have to have some more stitches," she decreed. "You will not need an anaesthetic if your breath is anything to go by."

Two days later I was discharged, or perhaps expelled would be a more suitable word. The final straw came when I placed my feet against a wall at the head of my bed and pushed mightily. The wheeled-bed shot across the floor partially demolishing a trolley containing medical what-have-you's before entangling itself with beds on the other side of the ward. Neither Sister nor Matron were much amused and an hour later saw me standing on Blackpool Station bound for Carlisle.

The train journey was uneventful apart from the surprise shown by two military policemen who were not over-impressed by a pilot officer wearing no head gear, bearing no identification and carrying a parachute over his shoulder. I arrived in the Mess late in the evening where I was royally greeted and celebrated by my pals. With the exception of Ken, these were the only people I had met in seven days who were genuinely pleased to see me.

McNT

The war years were peculiar in as much as one's unit with comrades was the only home available. Living quarters and the Mess were not 'home' but the Squadron or Flight was. A wicker work chair and feet on the stove was refuge from the belligerent world. When not flying, other pilots would discuss experiences and tactics while the poster-adorned crew room walls were a constant reminder of the correct way to shoot at the enemy or what to do if shot down in enemy territory. A great deal of reading was done either for instruction or relaxation.

Three hours flying a day was normal and this took up a lot of time, as preparation and after-landing procedures had also to be taken into account. Some blind flying was to be endured on the Link Trainer and parachutes and dinghies had to have periodical inspections. Pilots were expected to carry out compass calibration and weapon alignment so there was never a dull moment.

In fact dull moments were few and far between, especially when interspersed with moments of sheer terror and I expect a certain amount of panic.

Many years later I received an enquiry from an Air Historian in Cumberland by name of Peter Connon. He was researching aircraft accidents in the North East of England, the statistics of which I appear to have made a notable contribution to.

Peter Connon advised me as to what he had discovered about the Hurricane forced landing and the Miles Master 'Prang'. Wing Commander W D David's Officer Commanding's remarks would undoubtedly have pleased me at the time, but closing fifty years later, remembering as I do, they appear to be the understatement of the year, but then, he had been misinformed that I had 160 hours 16 minutes experience on Master aircraft so I expect he thought I might have done better if I had tried.

For your interest my cards read as follows:

01.11.42 P/O N H Berryman 127882 Hurricane I P2993, Exercise ?, Pilot's Experience ? At Gilsland, Cumberland 11.00 hrs Damage Cat B. Aircraft force-landed wheels up in field. Pilot injured after engine failure in flight. OC – Fracture in cylinder block caused severe glycol leak. Good force-landing under difficult conditions.

13.11.42 P/O N H Berryman 127882 Master I N8071 55 OTU, X-Country Ex, 160 hrs 16 on type. Annan airfield 09.35 hrs Damage Cat B. Tyre burst on take-off and aircraft ran through some rough ground causing damage to the undercarriage and propeller. OC -Consider pilot did all he could in the circumstances.

I was happy to be out of hospital and wanted to get into the air quickly. I was flying a Hurricane again on the 8th November, seven days after the accident. Fitness was largely up to the individual and I insisted I was fit. The mouth heals quickly and I bear few visible signs of injury. Aerobatics were not comfortable as the pressure of blood was increased in my head. The oxygen mask was uncomfortable to wear and a formation flight to 32000 feet with the intense cold and use of oxygen proved painful, but for every day 'stooging around' I could get by and was improving every day.

Friday 13th November was to be another memorable day. Asked to do an air test on a wretched Miles Master attached to the Flight, I taxied out, carried out cockpit checks, received a green light from the airfield controller and began a take off run.

I always considered the Master to be under powered and held the aircraft down on the runway to obtain plenty of speed for a climb. Just before I lifted off, there was a bang and the aircraft swung hard to right leaving the runway and digging a furrow in the grass with the starboard oleo leg. The aircraft wheel was no longer attached and neither was a foot of the starboard wing tip. Although I was by now crossing the airfield at 45 degrees to the runway I managed to lift the Master clear of the ground and with full throttle started to climb.

My intention was to do a circuit and land with retracted undercarriage, a manoeuvre I was by now quite accustomed to. Clever as the idea was, the operation was defeated when I saw a large hangar looming up between me and the skyline. With not a hope in hell of getting over the top of the hangar, I literally thumped the Master back onto the ground and closed the throttle.

The aeroplane was still skidding in a half circle at some speed as it passed between a line of Hurricanes attached to the Gunnery Flight, across the perimeter track and slid to a smoking crumpled halt on the Apron to the Maintenance Hangar. Before I could get out, a cycle and rider appeared. I recognised the figure climbing towards me immediately, it was P/O Charles Lawrence, one of my new-found friends from Terrell.

LANDING

DREAMING OF YOUR SWEETIE-HEART
WILL NOT LOWER YOUR UNDER-CART;
IF YOU FORGET YOUR FLAPS, OLD BEAN,
IN THE FAR-SIDE DITCH YOU'LL SOON BE SEEN
SITTING IN A TANGLED MOUND
OF HURRICANE, YOU IDLE HOUND.

Sent to me by my brother Alan after my Hadrian's Wall incident.

The shock of the crash had disturbed my vocal chords some-what and in a very high pitched voice I began to answer his questions as to what had happened. With greatcoat collar turned well up against the bitter wind and his service cap perched above his mass of curly hair, Charles with his usual helpful attitude listened stone facedly before interrupting with the sage pro-nouncement "Bullshit". This was his usual acknowledgement to any situation he did not fully understand. I was completely unscathed and after filling out an accident report form, I cycled off to lunch, returning to fly a Hurricane in the afternoon.

It was assumed that a burst tyre was the cause of the accident and nobody ever mentioned the matter to me again. I always had a feeling that there was more to the affair than was said and that a certain amount of 'cover up' reports had to be made by main-tenance personnel, so I consoled myself with the very last entry in the only diary I have ever kept. It reads, "Lucky or unlucky 13th – the third time will have to be very lucky!" There was never a third time, although I was to have some hairy moments, I never actually crashed another aircraft.

Charles, Paul, Ray and I found that we were being drawn closer than ever before. Constantly in the air together or in pairs, we worked to perfect a fighting technique and learned from each other's mistakes. We flew in all sizes of formation at all heights. We flew camera gun exercises, low level exercises and endless dog fighting.

A dog fight would start with two pilots flying in close forma-tion. At an agreed signal each would break away, climb or dive, hide in a cloud or perhaps dive low over the water. The objective was to catch your adversary unawares and in such a position that the camera gun set in the Hurricane's wing would 'shoot him down'.

Whatever may have been previously written, it is fact that fighter pilots never found deflection shooting easy for a variety of reasons. Some of the 'Aces' were better at it than the majority, but in the main, the enemy were shot down by attacking fighters three hundred yards dead astern and a three second burst of machine gun or cannon fire 'right up the arse'. We all got 'shot down' in turn, but occasionally when Ray McNair-Taylor and I were duelling, Ray would lose contact and I was able to see he was confused and searching the skies for me.

Sooner or later his RT would crackle up and a voice would enquire "Where are you Red 2?" I used to delay my reply until my camera gun was whirring away. The reply was always the same "I'm on your tail". To his amused chagrin, I was always "on his tail". The phrase became a joke and until his death, all correspondence concluded with those words. Today his son, David, and I use the same phrase if I wished to convey that 'I am right behind you'.

Sqn. Ldr. 'Jas' Storrar was O.C. gunnery flight, a man of humour and a great personality.

He had learned the fighter trade the hard way in the Battle of Britain, flying with 145 Squadron, and by November 1940, he had notched up 15 confirmed 'kills' flying the Hawker Hurricane.

As new boys, we listened avidly to his advice and instruction. His efforts were largely wasted on me, however, as my marksmanship was not deemed to be of the best. Frustrated no doubt, to wring some sort of ability out of me, he took me to one side and quite firmly spelled out the fact that if I did not show improvement with my guns the following few days, I certainly was not going to be posted to a fighter squadron. Determinedly I mounted my Hurricane the next day to attack a drogue towed by a Miles Martinet, and meeting the 'target' over the Solway Firth, began a series of attacks which hopefully would prove that I could aim straight. Starting with deflection shots of about 45 degrees, I grew increasingly enthusiastic, urged on no doubt by the intoxicating smell of cordite penetrating the cockpit from the eight .303 machine guns. By the time the exercise was nearly completed, I was so enthused, that I was breaking away so close to the drogue, I was well nigh astern of the Miles Martinet, the occupants of which could well have been terrified by my method of attack, as I was breaking every damn rule in the book in order to put some shots into the drogue.

As it was, however, suddenly the-drogue whistled over my cockpit cover and fluttered forlornly into the Solway Firth – never to prove evidence of my unerring marksmanship. I had hit the towing wire with some bullets. 'Jas' never queried the fact that I must have at least hit something, and apart from a rueful grin, assessed me as "Average" and a shake of the head.

'Jas' was only 2 years and 3 months older than I, but his baptism of fire in the Battle of Britain separated us immeasurably. In the bar, he was the first to buy me a pint, and this together with his added good humour and advice, served to change my attitude to war, and in so doing, I am sure put me on a path that with luck, I could survive.

After 1942, I saw 'Jas' only once more. At the opening of the Battle of Britain Memorial at Capel le Ferne by H.M. Queen Elizabeth the Queen Mother, the rain literally fell out of the sky, and I took refuge in my car while the rain continued to torrent. Suddenly, a young man knocked on the side window – "Please sign my book", he said holding out a rather wet volume, "I'm not a Battle of Britain pilot" I shouted, "You flew Spitfires" he said "that will suffice". I wound down the window, took the book and signed my name. Immediately above, I spotted the signature of 'Jas Storrar'. "Where did you get that", I shouted. "From the gent in the Jaguar next to you", he said, 'the one with the registration plate JAS". Regardless of the pelting rain, I ran to the Jag and the driver wound down his window. "Hello" he said, when did we last meet?" I was pleased to reply "At 32,000ft over Newcastle, Sir". They don't often come as good as 'Jas'. A good boss of 65, 165 and 234 Squadrons and a D.F.C. and Bar.

Early in December, Ray wanted to purchase a dog. This was a quite impractical thing to do, but he was a charming impractical man and older than I by five years. I went with Ray to a Dumfries farm to buy an English Springer Spaniel. Together we looked at the litter and fell hook, line and sinker for a dog which he immediately christened 'Macenty' (McNT). On the way home by train we decided to share responsibility for the 7-week-old pup, so that if either of us 'Got the Chop' (which was a nice way of saying getting killed) the other would take over full responsibility. Arriving at Annan Railway Station we mounted the RAF cycles we had deposited there.

Ray was a terrible cyclist and with a wriggling puppy and a plucked chicken tucked in his greatcoat his cycling ability became even worse. Although I was encumbered by a small ham, I eventually relieved him of the pup and chicken and we got back to our billets, Ray rather muddy as he had fallen off several times.

It was very cold and what coal we could fuel the tiny fires with was usually stolen from the coal pound. So cold was it one night that a surprised batman found Ray and me huddled together in one bed under a pile of our combined blankets. He probably thought the situation a bit queer, but we did not and we were at least warm, and so we continued towards Christmas 1942.

MAKE YOUR CHOICE

The course was due to end on 31st December and the flying intensified. Knowing that January would find me on an operational squadron, I wrote the following letter, which I found in my father's deed box upon his death. I am unable to say how it arrived there and I reproduce it unashamedly, as it serves to amplify the affection the family held for one another. Addressed to Mr and Mrs R W Berryman, and marked 'NOT TO BE POSTED', the letter began:

Thursday 10th December 1942

My Dear Mum, Dad and Alan,

This letter may never be posted, I hope not with all my heart, but I feel that now that flying is my job in earnest, for the time being anyway, that I should have a few words written somewhere where they will reach you if anything were to happen to me.

I love life dearly, and I suppose I am a little afraid, but if by giving my life I can do anything towards final victory for England (you know I would do so a thousand times) I shall go out the way I wish to.

You are the finest Mother and Father a chap could have, you have always done your utmost to help me, and I am eternally grateful. Young Bill is a good loyal brother and I only hope and pray that he will never have to go into the forces to go to war. I want young Alan to have every single thing of mine. Money, bonds and all private property. He can do with it what he pleases. Betty is to have some little thing of mine if she wishes.

Thank you again for everything you have ever done,

With fondest love, your loving son and brother,

Neville.

A year later on the 11th January 1944, before departing for overseas, I added another sheet from which I extract:

Thank you all again for another year of kindness. You mean such a lot to me and I thank God we have always been such a happy family. I sometimes wish that I had a little boy of my own, who could carry on and live my life, perhaps, where I leave off.

Cheerio and God Bless you all,

Nick.

Well, those letters never had to be posted, but before the next three years were out, I found one or two similar letters in the effects of my friends, two of whom died in their Hurricanes on the night of December 27th somewhere up in the mountains, the peaks of which I had so recently managed to avoid.

Christmas brought little respite from the intensity of the flying programme and with the exception of Christmas Day there was little jollity.

55OTU Commanding Officer was Wing Commander W D David, one of Britain's Fighter Aces. At the end of the war he was officially credited with 20 kills. Hearing a couple of us shooting our mouths off about Hurricanes in the bar, he smiled as he informed us that he would be able to run rings round us using a Gloucester Gladiator, the pre-war fighter, and we challenged him to prove it. He did, in no uncertain manner. Can it be wondered that I became humble.

In retrospect, the challenge offered to W.D.D. with a bravado that a mixture of youth and alcohol produced, was a bit unwise to say the least, for although 3 pairs of untrained eyes in Hurricanes searched the clouds the following morning for the boss in his Gladiator, from nowhere he appeared behind us bellowing over the RT that if we continued to be so carelessly unobservant, we each would be more of a liability to a squadron than an asset, and he managed to convey that message in about four words. So when I left 55 O.T.U. my assessment was once again, just 'AVERAGE FIGHTER PILOT'.

Dennis David had joined the R.A.F. in 1938 just in time to convert to Hurricanes with 87 Squadron. After many hairy moments during the battle for France when he destroyed 11 enemy aircraft, he was awarded a D.F.C. and Bar in just a few days. Then with 213 and 152 Squadrons, he became a "Wingco" at 23 years of age. Later, he flew in the Western Desert and the Far East against the Japs. Then he was awarded an A.F.C. and a C.B.E. He totted up 20 kills, was a great leader of men, loved his dogs, as did so many fighter pilots of those days.

When he invested in a greyhound called FLASH HARRY, a few of his R.A.F. associates shared in quite a few remunerative wins. In this man's presence, it was easy to become humble.

The course finished as planned on the last day of the year. Pilots were asked to specify a preference as to future occupation. Charles Lawrence and I, both devotees of the Hurricane, asked to go to a Hurricane Bomber Squadron, 'Hurrybombers'. Ray decided that a Spitfire Squadron was his choice and Paul, finding there was a post within the Operational Training Unit itself, opted to stay.

Ray and Charles were sent to newly-formed Typhoon squadrons, Paul got his wish and stayed at Annan, while I departed to a Spitfire squadron – so much for choice.

I have little doubt that I, together with my fellow fighter fledglings, climbed into an air force bus to be transferred to the railway station at Carlisle and sang our hearts out for the half hour journey, our songs were invariably bawdy and mostly covered the subject of manliness and bravery. One that comes to mind was:

I don't want to join the Air Force
I don't want to go to War
I'd rather hang around Piccadilly Underground
Living on the earnings of a High Born Lady.

I don't want a bullet up my 'arsole'
I don't want my bollocks shot away
I'd rather live in England, Merry, Merry England
And fornicate my bleeding life away.

All of this of course to cover up what we all felt – Trepidation.

THE CENTURION

No 66 Squadron, then at Ibsley just North of Ringwood, Hampshire, was to be my first operational squadron.

Before leaving the subject of 55 OTU Annan I must relate a series of strange events pertaining to that part of the country. 55 OTU was so-named because it was situated on the 55 degree North Line of Latitude, as does Hadrian's Wall.

After my second near miss with death in 13 days, one or two of my friends began joking about a mythical centurion of the Roman Army who patrolled the 55th parallel and who desired me as company in his lonely environment. The Centurion missed me in 1942 but was reminding me of his presence again thirty years later.

In 1972 my son Nicholas was serving in the RAF in Germany and, in order to keep his daughter Victoria amused, old air maps with plain white backs were cut up and used for scribble and crayon drawing.

I was delighted to receive my first communication from my grand-daughter which was quite unintelligible, and on the reverse side of a one foot square of map. I read her message to me and was reminded of my old friend once again as I found myself looking at the map on the other side. There, centre bottom, was Gilsland. Funny that Victoria should use that square, I thought.

That same year the Royal Navy asked me to go to Stranraer in my capacity of RNR Communications Officer. Wishing to travel by road with my Springer Spaniel, Bodger (who had taken over from McNT), I borrowed my wife's brand new Ford Capri. I had a wonderful journey North with Bodger at my side.

On the Carlisle by-pass the car stopped dead. It took me two hours to find and rectify the fault – a burnt out ignition condenser. The unusual fault could have happened anywhere, but why the 55th parallel?

Ten days later I was standing in the bar of my RN accommodation chatting to two RAF Officers. They were also staying at the hotel and had arrived to do a survey flying a Canberra out of West Freugh nearby. After a few beers, seeing that I was a uniformed flyer and having been regaled by a few of my RAF stories, I was invited to join them for the next morning trip.

Very early in the morning I was phoned to return to the RN Headquarters in Stranraer Castle as they had a communication problem. Before leaving the hotel, I slipped a note under the RAF Officers' door – "Sorry, unable to join you," I wrote. "The Navy needs me. May I take a 'rain check'?"

I had told the aviators about my 'Centurion' the previous evening, so I was hardly surprised when at lunch the next day, still looking decidedly shaken, they recounted how an engine had caught fire after take off. They had been lucky to get the Canberra landed again, and 'NO', they would rather I did not take them up on the 'rain check'. When you have time, just check up on which line of parallel West Freugh lays. I suspect the Centurion gave up then, as I have only had a minor brush with him since.

In 1980, retired from the RNR, I was surprised to get a communication from the Naval Secretary in Whitehall. The forthcoming NATO Exercise was short of a Fishery Control Officer at West Hartlepool, and would I go? I accepted, as I needed the money. Towards the end of the exercise, the Captain of the HQ Unit became distraught when his official transport broke down and he would be late for a top conference in Newcastle. As Fishery Control, I was not overworked and a visit to North Shields was an impending duty. I suggested to the Captain that if he would authorise payment for mileage, I would take him and still get him there on time.

It was a fast journey and my senior was delighted with the comfort of my Peugeot 504 and the expert driving of his junior officer. He was even more delighted when I pulled up outside HMS Caledonia on the banks of the Tyne with three minutes to spare before the conference started.

"Pick you up at 16:00 Sir," I called as he hurried away. Thinking I would check a map before proceeding to North Shields I switched off the engine.

From beneath the car came an ominous 'clang'. Inspection showed the rear exhaust pipe had parted company with the silencer. Yes, it could have happened anywhere and anytime, but why, when I am in uniform again, in Newcastle, on that bloody 55th parallel? That guy must reckon I owe him something.

Reverting to 1943 however, 66 Squadron was a long way from 'The Wall'. Mind you, they were just about to cross that Northerly deadly line for the only time in 27 years of commissioning. Due for a 'rest' period, they left in the following month for Sumbrugh in the Shetlands. If I had gone with them I am sure my Spitfire V would have stopped flying long before it got there.

In the January, however, there were two good reasons why I should never have been attached to 66. When S/Ldr Bird-Wilson 'The Boss' saw me land a Spitfire for the first time, he could probably have thought of three!

Statistically though there were only two, one being that I was not due for a 'rest' and two, my breathing, due to nose damage, was still very painful at high altitude and that was where the squadron was mainly operating. Flying Fortresses were carrying out daylight bombing operations against Brest, Lorient and St Nazaire and needed fighter protection. 66 went with them often.

Another factor became apparent to me also. I was a Hurricane trained pilot flying with experienced Spitfire chaps and, whilst any fighter pilot should be able to fly any fighter, it takes a considerable number of hours to be able to 'fight' with a new type. There were more newly-trained Spitfire pilots than Hurricane pilots anyway and it would have been more sensible if I had been sent to fly the New Hawker Typhoon.

The Hurricane and Typhoon, both designed by Sidney Camm of Hawker Aircraft Company, had many similarities. While

Hurricane and Spitfire are always mentioned in the same breath, they were as different to fly as chalk from cheese.

Without going into detail I can best explain by giving a comparison. Flying a Hurricane was like driving a Ford Escort 1.3 and the Spitfire like driving a Fiesta XR3. If you know more about horses than cars, the comparison would be a good point-to-point nag with a 10-to-1 Grand National runner. Both did a superb job and both saw service in every theatre of war from 1939 to 1945.

The squadron was over-established when they left for the Shetlands and I like to think that 'Birdy' Wilson sincerely meant 'Good Luck' and not 'AND GOOD LUCK' when he signed my log book for the last time.

'Birdie' knew just how important good luck could be. Early in his R.A.F. career, he had survived a bad crash when his co-pilot had perished. Then his luck nearly ran out when he clashed with the Luftwaffe ace Adolph Galland over London during the Battle of Britain in a 17 Squadron Hurricane. Birdie was no mean pilot, he had triumphed over 6 German attackers previously, but Adolph was another kettle of fish. Shot out of the sky and burning, he became one of Sir Archibald McIndoe's first "Guinea Pigs", and with a new nose, went on to claim another 5 German aircraft, downed whilst leading 152 and 66 Squadrons, and after leading Spitfire and Mustang wings before WWII ended. His uniform bore the ribbons of a D.F.C. and Bar, a D.S.O. and an A.F.C. and Bar, a Dutch D.F.C. and a Czechoslovak Medal of Merit. How lucky I was to be initiated into squadron operations by such a man.

THE LADY DEFIANT

Posted to Warmwell near Dorchester I thought 257 Squadron Typhoons would be awaiting me, but I was wrong. A rapid welcome from Wing Commander Douglas, the Station Commander, saw me in a WAAF-driven Jeep heading for the South East corner of the all-grass airfield.

"What do 276 Squadron do?" I asked the WAAF.

She gave a naughty grin as she replied, "Fornicate, the same as 263 and 257 if they get the chance, Sir."

I had not long to wait for the real answer. In front of the hangar, bearing a 276 squadron notice board, stood three Boulton & Paul Defiants and two Supermarine amphibian Walruses. "Hell," I thought, "What's all this?"

I had arrived at 'A' Flight 276 Air Sea Rescue Squadron. It was a large Squadron with other Flights at Harrowbeer, North of Plymouth, and Portreath on the West Cornish Coast, and Fairwood Common South Wales. It was commanded by S/Ldr Ronnie Hamlyn, a Battle of Britain pilot whose boast was to have shot down five enemy aircraft before breakfast.

There was a modicum of truth in the story. On the 24th August 1940, Ronnie Hamlyn, a Sergeant Pilot at the time, was on a disciplinary charge for landing a Spitfire with retracted under-carriage. Whilst being reprimanded by the Group Captain Station Commander of Biggin Hill the order came to Scramble. Making his excuses he scrambled and promptly shot down an ME 109 followed by a bomber later on that day. His showing that day, and later on shooting down three more 109s, earned him a DFC. Now as a Squadron Leader he had been awarded an AFC for his work with Air Sea Rescue, which he wore with the DFM.

Each of the Flights had a Flight Commander and, in the case of 'A' Flight, this was F/Lt Jimmy Renvoise. A chat with Renvoise told me my role in the set up. As a pilot officer I was his No. 2 and I was to fly a Defiant in searching the seas for ditched airmen. I had heard about the Defiant and I was not elated at the thought of the job.

If the Hurricane was a point-to-point nag, this was a dray horse. Larger than the Hurricane but powered by the same engine, it carried a Browning four machine-gun powered turret weighing one ton, which was operated by an air gunner. I was relieved to hear this, as it seemed a considerable distance from the office up front (cockpit) to the turret amidships.

Introduction to flight in this aeroplane was about as exciting as a middle-aged spinster wearing woolly drawers. Once in the air it was comfortable and stable. Getting it into the air was the problem. I soon worked out that the safest way was to hold it on the ground until it was possible to see the berries in the airfield boundary hedge, lift off and tuck the undercarriage away fast. Then not attempting to gain height until 160 mph appeared on the clock, when a gentle climb could be attempted.

As soon as a pilot was accustomed to this new approach to aviation, the ground crew attached two smoke floats and a bomber type 'Lindholme' dinghy to the underside of the wing, then the air gunner got in. All this was in case the first tussle with the Defiant had been too easy.

Operationally the Defiant had never been a success. Apart from one glorious day when the Luftwaffe attacked what they thought to be Hurricanes, only to find a lot of rear firing Brownings rattling away at them. Word soon got round the enemy fighters that there was a 'sting in the tail', and from then on Defiants were shot out of the sky.

Patrolling or searching in the middle of the English Channel so equipped, was not what I considered to be the answer to longevity, but sometimes we were given a Spitfire escort. I worked out my own method of survival if attacked; no turning in ever decreasing circles for me, just throttle wide open and head for the shores of England so low over the water that the prop blades spun the surface into a trailing spume. With a continual gentle weave, it would take a very good FW 190 pilot to get a bead on me. I knew from experience that looking through a gun sight and flying that low did not go together.

My own cleverness, however, nearly caught me out one evening and the shore defences did not pick up my IFF Identification signal as I sped homewards, very low as usual. Above and in front of me I saw two Spitfires coming fast on interception. Fortunately they recognised the Defiant shape before opening fire and soon I had a Spitfire on each wing tip formating on me. I recognised them as 312, the Czechoslovakian Squadron, by their markings D U. I was glad of their company until they gently eased in and alternately tipped my wings with theirs, and this at twenty feet. I froze and flew dead straight, not daring to even glance left or right. The Canadian Air Gunner Sgt Frisby, who was normally verbose, subsided into a grave-like silence. Funny chaps the Czechs; some used to go to bed in hair nets.

February and March went quickly. The job was new to me and there was plenty to learn and practice. The idea of dog fighting in the Defiant against anything the Germans were likely to put into mid-Channel was out of the question, and now low cloud was more a friend than foe.

Sometimes low flying over the sea became difficult as the mists and cloud merged with the sea, confusing the horizon. Conditions which my colleagues F/Sgt Hall and F/Sgt Elder had just discovered. Returning from a search in an area South of Portland Bill, they ran into poor weather and whilst attempting to cross the 600 ft high hills surrounding Dorchester, found themselves amongst the high tension power cables. Short of petrol, Hall could not take the longer but safer way to base (via Poole Harbour, over Wareham and follow the railway line). A route I favoured and always used in bad weather. Anyway, seeing the power cables and obviously shaken, Hall yanked back the stick and climbed into cloud again, hollering out to Bill Elder, his gunner, to bale out.

In a split second he was over the side, leaving Bill still scrabbling about on the floor for his chest-type parachute which had to be clipped to his harness before going out himself. Not exactly an enviable position to be in, as knowing the Defiant, it would by this time have been heading for the ground at a fast rate of knots. Built like a Brick Out-House, they had that tendency. Bill got out at 1500 feet and landed seconds later, literally on top of the legendary figure of the 'Giant of Cerne Abbas' cut out of the chalk hillside. It may still be seen from the roadside if you are travelling in that area. A fearsome figure, naked and well equipped and armed with a club, a piece of equipment only outshone for size by his John Thomas.

When Bill got back little the worse physically for his adventure, we ribbed him somewhat as to what part of the anatomy he had actually touched down upon. Hall was okay but very shocked, and distressed when found. Bill Elder dared mention a few days leave to recover and was dressed down by Jimmy Renvoise and threatened with an LMF addition to his documents of service record. They were both flying the next day.

When the stimulus of meeting new people in new surroundings had worn off, I was not too certain that I enjoyed being an Air Sea Rescue (ASR) pilot. I had been trained as, and I felt like, a fighter pilot. I knew what it was like to twist the gun button to fire and unleash eight machine guns and breathe the exciting smell of cordite. Now I could not fight back with any hope of success. There would be no point in being a dead hero especially as nine times out of ten there was nobody around to even notice the splash.

However, the RAF had given me a commission and a decent bed. My pay was 13s 6d a day and this was probably enough to consider purchasing the motor cycle I had never managed to get. I had no choice in the matter anyway, so I continued to drag the Defiant round the sky whilst my companions in the Mess took fiendish delight in formating on me in the 257 Squadron Typhoons or 263 Squadron Whirlwinds, before peeling off with panache and the usual two fingered salute.

There was a task to be done meanwhile and it was more than rewarding to spot a dinghy in the grey seas after a lengthy search. The drill on sighting was to drop a smoke float near to the unfortunate in the water and then to follow this with the large dinghy and supplies. All this as well as trying never to take your eyes from the dinghy, as in poor visibility they could often disappear again. A climb to 1500 feet to transmit a fix in order that shore bases could get a bearing on the Defiant, then with luck the Walrus or the Rescue Launches would be on their way. If I was short of fuel I would ask for relief aircraft to take over the vigil. Mostly it would be two sections of Spitfires who would be scrambled to relieve me of the responsibility, as by now the

German shore stations could also have picked up the radio transmission.

If the weather was reasonable and the seas not too rough the Walrus would arrive first. That too would require protection, for the days of chivalry were long gone. It was a wonderful sight to see the ungainly Walrus thump down into the water throwing a mountain of salt spray and then taxi to the beleaguered airmen. I seldom saw the boats arrive on the scene as I couldn't afford to hang around that long! Maybe not as glamorous a job as I should have liked but rewarding it certainly was.

1943 produced a beautiful Spring and the Dorset countryside and meandering rivers repaid the weather in full by dressing in their best. The Officers' Mess was at West Stafford two miles from the airfield. Stafford House, a magnificent grey stone country house, completed my contentment by offering me good shelter, food and company.

As I have already mentioned, the Czechoslovakian Spitfires were about and 312 Squadron officers were here. I often found it difficult to suppress a smile as I watched those elegant men in silk dressing gowns (hair coiffured, pomanded and netted) trip off up the beautiful winding panelled staircase towards bed, often scenting the air behind them with fragrances that Harrods perfumery would have envied. It was an anachronism that these beings were the same as the unsmiling courageous pilots I should meet in the air on the morrow.

In 1940, Warmwell had suffered badly from several bombing raids when there was considerable loss of life and damage to buildings. It seemed unlikely that there would be a recurrence of the tragedy as now the airfield and surrounding towns were protected by 257 Squadron Typhoons. Always in the daylight hours, two aircraft with bored novel-reading pilots ensconced, sat facing the prevailing wind ready to scramble upon sight of a white Very light sailing skywards from the Watchtower.

In seconds, with a bang and a roar, seven tons of fighter plane would hurtle skyward. The beautiful Whirlwinds of 263 Squadron were there to carry the war to the enemy, loaded as they were with bombs and cannon. The Westland Whirlwind was an aircraft never exploited to its fullest potential. Two underslung Rolls Royce Peregrine engines were not powerful enough to do it justice. Merlin engines would have sufficed, but production of these never exceeded the insatiable demand of Bomber Command, and many a Whirlwind pilot's life was lost in consequence.

With so many different types of engines and airframe to maintain, my undying admiration went to the ground crews who soldiered on in all weathers to keep the aircraft serviceable. Their knowledge was great and their hearts twice as big.

I remember having a bit of a showdown with a fitter one evening. I had landed an aircraft with a faltering engine and I wanted it back on line the following morning. I gave instructions in the absence of 'Chiefy' the engineer flight sergeant. When the fitter complained that he had no rest for twelve hours, I unfairly bombasted him and left him with the parting shot, "All right then, get some bloody sleep and kill me in the morning." We were short of serviceable aircraft and if there had been a 'flap', I might easily have had to take it off. The aircraft was checked and repaired by first light. I made a point of thanking the crew, and I felt a right sod.

The WAAF too, were great. Warmwell had a lot of them. They were evident in every department; Headquarters, Accounts, Stores, Parachute Section, Drivers, Cooks, Batwomen and Waitresses. There was not a lot they were not into and although their uniforms were not over complimentary to the female shape, they never stopped being women.

I was privileged in the fact that I shared a Batwoman with two other officers (both incidentally Burmese), F/O Kim and F/O Yeo. 257 Squadron was the Burmese Squadron and they were both Typhoon pilots. The Batwoman's name was Jeanie MacPherson and she was a very large lady in every way. Aged 20, she hailed from Edinburgh, and she would not tolerate any mucking about. She made no bones about the fact I was her favourite, and cared for me like a mother.

I never had to think about clothes or uniform and she kept me immaculate. At the same time she fiercely defended my reputation if any of the other girls started to tittle tattle. She always seemed to be there, especially if I was tired, and a cup of tea and a smile was always available.

She could be just as sharp with her tongue if she thought I had transgressed from her puritan outlook on life.

As an ASR pilot I never knew when the next call would come. It was a 'watch on stop on' job, as we were not over established with Defiant pilots and there was always an Immediate and a Thirty Minute Readiness aircraft available.

One evening I landed in the dark. I was the only officer there at the time and a sergeant had thoughtfully telephoned the Mess to order me an Operational Breakfast, knowing I had missed dinner. OB was egg and bacon, an unusual treat reserved for aircrew who missed meals through operations.

It had been a long fruitless search and I was tired and dirty when I arrived at the Mess. In the bar I could hear sounds of merriment, but I was in no mood for jollity. I just needed bed. I should at least have washed, but I was too tired for that even. I went into the Dining Room. It was silent and in darkness, so I pushed through the swing doors into forbidden territory, the Kitchens.

My Hello produced an answer from amidst the ranges and sinks. It was a WAAF who answered me, standing near a range with one shoe on. The other shoe was poised in her left hand. In her right she held a blacking brush. Obviously she was 'bulling' her shoes up.

"Who is the Duty Cook?" I questioned.

"Right here," she replied, "are you the Operational Breakfast?" My affirmative produced an immediate reaction. She dropped the shoe brush, pulled a mob cap over her upswept hair and at the same time did a hop and a skip towards the hot range, pushing a large frying pan over the heat. She had her back to me and I was faintly amused at the girl. One shoe on and one off, with wisps of mousy brown hair sticking out from the back of her cap.

It was a stupid thing to do, as fraternisation between officers and WAAF was frowned upon, but I pushed her loose hair back under her hat. She stiffened as I gazed at her slender white neck disappearing into a white overall. She wore no shirt. Round her neck was a gold chain with a small cross resting at the top of her bosom.

She turned to look at me. I must have looked terrible, as an oxygen mask always left its outline of dirt around nose and mouth. She lifted her face and swung her arms up and around my neck, one hand still holding a black shoe. We kissed. It was a long warm kiss and I felt the blood run hot in my chest. Before I could repeat the operation, there was the sound of footsteps beyond the swing doors. We broke away from each other like naughty children. I turned towards the dining room and she to the frying pan.

I was sitting in semi-darkness in the deserted dining room when she came in with a plate, which she put before me.

"That was nice," I said.

"Lovely," she replied, wrinkling her nose and turning away. I could hear distant laughter from the bar as I picked up a knife and fork. I glanced down at the plate.

"Oh good," I thought, "Two eggs!" That was the nice thing about WAAFs. Whatever the job, they never stopped being women.

THE UGLY DUCKLING

Within a few days I was involved in a sortie that was to have considerable influence on my future life, as without this occurrence I would undoubtedly have continued as a single-engine fighter pilot with the accompanying consequences. The war was only about a year away from D-day and the invasion of the continent by the Allies.

Jimmy Renvoise had taken a day's leave as his wife was visiting and the date was April 4th. The shrill sound of the telephone at the door of my room awoke me before 6:00 am. An excited W/O Bird was on the other end of the line from the Sergeants Mess. He was readiness Walrus pilot and he had been ordered to take off. A Spitfire pilot was in the drink but because of sickness he was a third member short in his crew. A Wireless Air Gunner he had, but no Gunner. Knowing I was the Thirty Minute Readiness Defiant pilot I told him to "get the show on the road, I could fire the bloody guns if necessary" and I was on the way!

The 'Shagbat' started rolling as I climbed in, shouting to Corporal Rowlands to make the Thirty Minute Defiant unserviceable. If Group wanted any more out there they would have to send some 'Spits', and we headed South-West towards France.

Soon over Portland and flying at 1000 feet, I settled into the second pilot's seat and watched Bird as he seduced the Walrus into heading in the right direction. I say that because until you got on first name terms with this aeroplane it had a tendency to waltz, and that is how it felt to the uninitiated. Bird was a seasoned hand with this girl however, and she settled to her job with a good natured thresh from her Pegasus engine. I was surprised to see that the Wop/AG behind me was my own gunner Sgt Frisby. I had not thought of it myself, but it was good reasoning to take a team, and 'Fris' was used to looking at the back of my head.

Twenty five minutes brought us into the search area and all eyes were riveted to the tumbling sea below. It was a cold April morning and Bird thought the sea strength about four, which would be all right for a landing. Half an hour of searching brought no success. It was like looking for a needle in a haystack. Then suddenly, there he was. Our hearts sank when we saw that he was floating in his Mae West life jacket and that no dinghy was in sight. We would have to hurry.

Bird dropped a smoke float, more to get wind direction than anything else. With a thump and a bang we were down and taxiing through the choppy water towards our friend in peril. God, we should have to get him out quickly.

I spotted him first, as by now I was standing in the front hatch. As we approached I threw a line. He made no attempt to take hold of it although his arms appeared to be flailing the water to gather it.

Knowing that seconds were precious and that it would take time to turn the Walrus to get closer, I leapt over the side with such vigour that the Port wing float cracked me over the head before it passed me by. For a second I was stunned, but not injured and I turned and struck out for the downed pilot.

I reached him and gasped out words of encouragement. His life jacket was not inflated so I delved about under water until I found the CO2 bottle release which I yanked down and was relieved to see him rise higher in the water as his life jacket filled with gas. I did the same for myself and felt happier with more buoyancy. Still he made no response. I was shocked to find him still wearing his parachute and dinghy. He was terribly heavy and it had to come off. I found the harness quick release box under the water, turned it and tried to strike the front plate. Not being able to use enough strength from the front, I got behind him and attempted to hit the box into the pit of the stomach. Still I could not exert enough force. I needed help and turned to signal the Walrus. My heart sank as I saw it turning and re-turning 150 yards away. Why in the name of Hell was he sodding about out there. I was here, with my friend, floating in a mass of fluorescent dye which oozed from my Mae West.

I returned to the problem of getting the parachute off. I was beginning to think this chap was a 'goner' as I had found not a flicker of life since my arrival. All the time I was aware of his shoulder flash on his battle dress floating up before my eyes, 'Australia' and his sergeant's stripes indicated his rank. By now I could feel the cold biting into my bones and the Walrus was no nearer. I realised then that I could see them but they could not see us in the tumbling waves.

I raised my arms high and shouted. Soon I got an answering wave. The Walrus with engine ticking over seemed to hurtle past as I grabbed the catapult mounting at water level, below the rear hatch.

The Australian weighed a ton under my left arm and I held on with my right. The Walrus surged on, dragging us both through the water. I released my hold on the aircraft as my lungs and nostrils started to fill with water. We were alone again. A second try to lift us out was better executed. Bird came at us more slowly and into wind. Once again I felt the underwater tow, and was exhausted. I released my grip again but was surprised to find myself hanging head down into the rear hatch. Frisby, using superhuman strength that is found only with desperation, had somehow hauled me in. I fell in a vomiting heap inside the hatch and they did another circuit for the Australian. I remember nothing of the ultimate take off and journey to base, only that I was shivering at about the same speed as the vibrating airframe. Frisby told me the Australian was dead.

I was able to get out of the Walrus unaided but felt sick and shaky. Leading Aircraftsman Unstead for once forgot about his ever mobile sweeping broom and handed me a steaming hot cup of tea. I laughed off a visit to the sick quarters and opted for a hot bath. Someone took me to the Mess and I made for my room, looking somewhat yellow as the fluorescent dye had coloured everything. I started down the corridor and came face to face with Jeanie McPherson as yellow sea water continued to drip from my sodden clothing onto her polished lino. Jeanie's face held a peculiar expression, one I had seen before somewhere.

"Where the devil have you been," she said. "Just look at your trousers!"

Ah yes, now I knew. That was not Jeanie standing there, it was Aunt Maude. I'm convinced she pushed me into a hot bath and washed me like a child but I could not swear to it. Three years later, as a guest at my wedding, she denied it anyway.

Thirty one years later in April 1974 as a Lieutenant RNR, I found myself alone on the bridge of a Ton Class mine sweeper while the 'professionals' took lunch. The sweeper was tossing its way towards Guernsey in windy weather on a post-refit trial and the sweeps were being towed astern.

I was joined on the bridge by an RN Captain of the trials inspection team. He took stock of the situation and admonished me for allowing the Sweep Deck men to work without life jackets. As a Lieutenant I made a policy of never arguing with Captains so lifting the microphone of the broadcast system I ordered, "Sweep Deck, Sweep Deck, wear life jackets, I repeat wear life jackets." Satisfied, the Captain went on to explain to me that any man who fell overboard would perish in twenty minutes. Unable to resist the temptation to be provocative I disagreed and we had a slight altercation on the subject.

Half an hour later the Captain and I were alone again at the lunch table. He had a reference book at his elbow. He eyed the medal ribbons on my chest and the wings on my sleeve and showing just a touch of humility said, "You were right, the book says, survival estimated 50 minutes. How did you know that?"

"I've been here before," I replied. "Fell in once April 1943. They pulled me out after 25 minutes and I was only half dead".

That evening he bought me a 'Horses Neck'.

But to return to 1943, the following morning I was none the worse for my ducking and reported to Flights as usual. A Group Captain arrived from 10 Group HQ at Rudloe Manor and he interrogated me, finishing with a complimentary remark about my efforts.

I was concerned about my wrist watch, the Bulova. Not waterproof, it was ruined. He told me to claim from the RAF for a replacement; I could have £2 13s. For now I settled by dropping the watch into the fluid of a broken compass bowl. Just before lunch, Jimmy Renvoise called me into his office.

"Be ready for flying in the 'Shagbat' at 2 o'clock," he said.

"I cannot," I replied. "I'm readiness on the Defiant."

Jimmie's rejoinder stopped me in my tracks. "You will not have to worry about that any more," he said. "I have to get you Operational on the Walrus as soon as possible."

That afternoon I piloted the Walrus for the first time when we took off for Poole Harbour and some sea landings. It appeared that my destiny was to pick aircrew out of the sea, not shoot them down into it.

The Bulova watch was packed off to my father in Chelsea, where he persuaded one of his customers, a watchmaker, to attempt a repair. I received it back within a month, no charge and with compliments. It is still ticking today and financially it stands me at the initial cost of ten dollars, less His Majesty's Government's donation of two pounds thirteen shillings. At four dollars to the pound then, I must be in pocket.

Before finally leaving this episode, I must tell of some inexplicable findings at the Public Records Office whilst verifying facts for this book.

An entry under 10 Group on that date records that, 'A Walrus of 276 Squadron with Spitfires of 616 and 504 Squadrons as escort, were searching for a 129 Squadron pilot'.

129 Squadron records that F/Sgt Symonds returning from an operation escorting 6 Whirlwind aircraft carrying out a shipping strike on Cherbourg, dived into the sea from 300 feet but an attending Air Sea Rescue Walrus was unable to effect a rescue owing to rough seas. In 276 Squadron records, Air 27/1597, it states Walrus L2335 was ordered to search position 160 degrees 40 miles. After search, pilot was located floating face downwards, Walrus landed on sea and endeavoured to get body of pilot on board – owing to the fact he was still wearing Mae West,

uninflated, parachute and harness, it was very difficult. In an attempt to get body into Walrus P/O Berryman went overboard but had to give up having exhausted himself.

Further enquiries as to the story of F/Sgt Symonds enlightens us to the fact that he was a Yorkshireman with apparently no connection with Australia whatsoever, and his name appears on the Royal Air Force Memorial at Runnymede, listed as 129 Squadron and lost on April 4th 1943.

Perhaps the only truth I have related refers to my conversation with the RN Captain in 1974. Whatever public records say, I certainly never saw an escorting Spitfire the whole of airborne time, and Symonds must have been wearing a colleague's battledress blouse. So much for history – but then, it was a pretty confusing war.

I flew the Defiant only twice more. Once on an air test and the last time on a delivery flight to Harrowbeer. Upon arrival I parked alongside a hanger and was asked to fly Spitfire P8325 back to Warmwell. 276 had teeth again, as the Spit had eight machine guns. As I arrived over Warmwell airfield I put on a bit of a show for Renvoise's benefit, just to remind him I was a Spitfire pilot.

The ruse worked, as eight days later I was piloting Spitfire AQ-C P8131 on a sea search for a Fortress crew. My No. 2 was Sgt McKay, one of a new batch of Canadians who had arrived especially to fly the Spitfires. The same month I was at Predannack on Bolt Head with Walrus 2282, on Standby to pick out any of the 60 US Air Corps Thunderbolt pilots who might drop in the Channel as they carried out one of their first sweeps over France. The Yanks were now in it up to their necks.

I was delighted as I now had the best of two worlds, and henceforth I flew the Spitfires and the Walruses, often in the same half day.

No two aircraft could be less alike, and their role just as different. I enjoyed the challenge. The Spitfires were re-furbished and bore the designation of MkIIc, specially equipped to carry internally a dinghy and a supplies container in the flare chutes. With eight machine guns, we could search and fight back if intercepted. Everyone felt a lot easier in mind.

It was this period of flying Defiants, Spitfires and Walruses, Lysanders and Tiger Moths that resulted in the "Spitfire on it's nose" episode – someone is bound to ask so I may as well come clean.

Off on a search, in a rush, No. 2 ready to go, I got a signal to stop from a fitter. Jimmy Renvoise ran up to the aircraft and told me to remove my collar and tie explaining pedantically that if I fell in the sea, my tie would shrink and choke me. What a time to bloody well tell me that, I thought. Of course he was right, and of course I knew the fact well. However, I was always a bit of a city gent even in the air and besides, my tie was secured by my lucky gold pin. He had to demand twice that I obeyed before I struggled under my parachute harness and Mae West to comply.

As mad as hell I threw collar, tie and pin at the fitter, gave my No. 2 the thumbs up for go, gunned the throttle to make a move and put AQ-D neatly up on its nose. That episode earned me a red endorsement in my log book "Carelessness!" After that I always carried my lucky tie pin even if I did not wear it.

As to operating the Walrus there surely never was an aircraft that performed so well under such difficult circumstances. My first experience with the old Shagbat was in Poole Harbour with Jim Renvoise as my instructor. After take-off I was asked to fly it to Poole. Fly we did, but only in the general direction of Poole. Walruses seemed always to recognise inexperience and whilst showing no direct malevolence to its new pilot, took pleasure in proceeding rather in its own style that what might be expected of it, coming from such a fine stable as Supermarine and being designed by Mitchell of Schneider Trophy and Spitfire fame. Consequently we waltzed our way towards Bournemouth, seemingly as much sideways as forwards.

By the time we arrived I had the feel for her and after a couple of water landings to the East of Brownsea Island I was invited to try a take-off and landing. In these sheltered waters I managed very well. For take-off control column right back, with the 'spectacles' wheel fully over to the right to hold the port wing out of the water, where it always rested. Increase throttle quickly to full, both hands on the column now, ease forward to bring the hull up on to the step, judging when to bring the port wing up, then gently back on the controls to lift off at around 65mph, with the occasional kick on rudders to correct any swing the waves would impart to straight take-off. For landing, a straight approach, throttle off at 75mph, round out and she did the rest herself. To any pilot 'a piece of cake'.

Within three days I was emulating these procedures off Lulworth Cove in rougher waters and progressed to the Tidal race one experiences off Portland Bill. A 'piece of cake' suddenly became a can of worms, as one fought like a maniac to control this beast as it leaped from wave top to wave top. Plunging into the troughs with uncontrolled thuds that shook the aircraft from nose to stern, constantly trying to entice this girl into the air. Then, pushing and pulling on the control column, rudders kicked violently left, right and left again, we would hit a wave top before flying speed was attained and the whole shebang would hurtle into the air, hang on the propeller for a second, then either bury her nose deep into a foaming roller that sent a deluge of water through the open cockpit top to engulf the radio operator in the rear or if you were lucky and clever at the same time the top of the next terrifying roller would be clipped and bounded from with just enough air speed to fly. Sometimes a really rough wave would twist you off course by 90 degrees.

Rough sea landings and take-offs certainly made one sweat. Either with exertion or fear, I know not, both I suspect. So badly did one attempt to take off go when on a rescue sortie, my crew threatened to take to the dinghy themselves.

All this rough treatment the dear Shagbat took with a smile. She certainly came from a good stable.

Alex Henshaw, Supermarine Test Pilot has written similar words about the Walrus in his book 'Sigh for a Merlin'. A far more experienced pilot than I could ever hope to be, I commend his Walrus experiences to your reading.

TOAD OF TOAD HALL

Sometimes personal tragedy entered my life. One bright morning I was standing on the edge of the airfield when two white Very lights (the signal for 'Scramble') hurtled skywards. I automatically turned to look at the Readiness Typhoons, their engines always warm so they would soon be away.

I was surprised to see no 'Tiffies' in their usual spot at the end of the East-West runway, but a loud roaring of engines from the direction of 257 Dispersal signified action somewhere. Quickly two Typhoons were tearing across the grass using a short runway more or less West-East. Caught with their pants down the two pilots were 'Scrambling' down-wind, in echelon port formation and not seeing a small Royal Naval aircraft approaching to land from the other direction. Too late, the control tower banged off a red warning signal and the next seconds were mayhem. The leading Typhoon, attempting to avoid the incoming aircraft, lifted off early and tried to turn to starboard and towards me. Without enough flying speed for such a manoeuvre the right wing stalled, hit the ground and the Typhoon cart-wheeled over and over and over again.

I started to run towards the tumbling aircraft as I saw the pilot thrown clear and tossed like a cork a hundred feet into the air. I was running so fast that the pilot hit the ground seconds before I reached him.

His safety straps had broken and in his parachute harness he lay in a crumpled heap, bloody and broken in every limb. I knelt down, drew my sheath knife from my flying boot, and started to cut into the harness.

His lips moved and his limbs twitched. I was horrified, but I had to do something. Bits of aircraft strewn about were smouldering and I felt so inadequate. I was grateful when the ambulance arrived and relieved me of the responsibility. My good friend F/Lt Dusty Miller mercifully died before arriving in hospital.

Jimmy Renvoise took one look at my face as I walked into the crew room and sent me on four days leave. Happy to have leave, I did not know where to go.

In the highly emotional state that I was, I knew it would be the wrong move to go to London and home, in case Mother sensed my temporary feelings of shock. I made a very wise decision and mounted my newly-acquired 1935 BSA 250 cc motorcycle and, like Toad, hit the exciting open road to Hereford, where I hoped to find Uncle Cyril and Aunt Maude (Ken's parents and Father's brother).

I had done little motorcycling and by the time I got to Bristol I was so buffeted and noisily bounced about that I made for the Railway station. Here a ticket for an Adult with accompanying luggage enabled me to continue in a more dignified manner.

Once at Hereford, I alighted from the train, mounted the BSA and made for 197 College Road as if I had travelled the whole distance by road. My Uncle and Aunt were delighted to see me and, to an intrepid pioneer motorcyclist like Cyril, I was not prepared to elucidate the details of the journey.

Fortune favours the brave, they say, and I was delighted to hear that Ken was at Credenhill, only five miles away. He was able to get away in the evenings and he introduced me to his friends.

Arriving at the main gate quite late one night, three passengers and I dismounted from the BSA. We had imbibed more than a few beers in Hereford taverns and my passengers were late and for the high jump.

The RAF Police Corporal in the Guardroom looked at me incredulously as I explained in a slightly slurred voice, that without the help of these brave airmen I would have been unable to quell a near-riot due to a punch up with the Army. He believed not one word of the story, but he was wise enough not to argue the toss with an unknown flying officer pilot. They stole into the camp and disappeared whilst I weaved my inebriated way through the country lanes back to Hereford. The following day a policeman on point duty in High Town stopped the traffic rather suddenly. The road was wet and I skidded, but deftly managed to lay the bike at his feet, where I sat looking up at the wet end of a cart horse.

The next day I set off with a 'Poop Poop' to the high road again, waving a flamboyant farewell, looking like Biggles himself. I drove a mile down the road and took the train back to Dorchester.

I never rode this motorcycle very well. Sometimes I closed the twist grip throttle the same way as one closes the throttle on a Spitfire, backwards. The resulting burst of speed when intending to slow down was often spectacular.

MY KINGDOM FOR A 'PLANE

In order that efficiency in rough sea landings was maintained on the amphibian, I sometimes made the practice sessions an excuse to get away to Cornwall where the food was particularly good. St Ives Bay was very near RAF Portreath and a night's rest there could mean two days of 'blindfolded wrestling' amongst the Atlantic rollers. Such an excursion brought me into professional contact with a WAAF Operations Officer named Susan Harris. Working in the Ops Room on the hill overlooking Portreath Harbour, she manned the Radio Telephone long enough to get me out of a spot of trouble amongst the balloon defence at Plymouth. Arriving safely at Portreath, I made a visit to Ops to find and thank the girl with the nice voice. She was 21, smallish and pretty, with twinkly blue eyes and always wearing her hair in a short pigtail tied with black ribbon. We liked each other immediately we met, decided that physical contact was better than professional and over a beer in the local pub began a love affair that for me has probably never finished, as I often think of her with great affection.

We spent time together whenever possible and as her duties were more regulated than mine, she journeyed to Warmwell whenever she could get two days off. The train trip from Cornwall was arduous but she had not far to go for accommodation when she arrived as I arranged for her to stay with the Station Master and his wife at Moreton Station. They were very kind to both of us and our meetings were fun. The chaps on the Squadron knew we were in the throes of young love and did everything they could to ease my workload and make her break from duty as long as possible. She could be strangely irresponsible and trusted in God to get her back to Portreath in time for duty. One last minute dash was made by Walrus, me piloting and Sue with her legs curled up in the second pilot's seat. Somehow I made this trip almost an operational necessity, as this Shagbat was due at Harrowbeer for a major inspection. By a long stretch of the imagination I found the cloud base at Harrowbeer too low for a safe approach, so I overflew and landed thirty minutes later at Portreath, where Susan was unceremoniously dumped on the end of the runway with a quick kiss and goodbye. A speedy return to Harrowbeer, where the cloud had miraculously cleared, enabled me to land, park the Walrus and hop into a Spitfire due for delivery to Warmwell. I landed forty minutes later just as darkness descended.

On another occasion, her trust in my Mr Fixit capabilities nearly came adrift. A trip was connived in the Squadron Tiger Moth, ostensibly to deliver some confidential documents. At the last minute our 'Tiger' went unserviceable. Undeterred, I rang 257 only to find that their Magister was away. A phone call to 263 dashed all hopes when they reported that they always borrowed 257's Magister. Susan looked at me with sorrowful blue eyes. This time she had cooked her goose. Sudden inspiration came to me. Target Towing Flight had a Miles Martinet, similar to a Master. I could fly those darned things. TT were helpful. No, I could not borrow the Martinet but I could have the loan of a Lysander if I could fly it.

"Fly it? Me, of course I could fly it. Yes please, I would be right over!"

I put the phone down, turned to the crew room in general and said "Which one of you guys can tell me about flying a Lysander?"

Warrant Officer Simmonds (renowned for his experimental engineering projects, like hot water systems for the ground crew, refrigerators for the wife and depth charges for fishing) came up with some information which I quickly digested and hoped like Hell it was more reliable than his experiments.

I dashed across to TT Flight and God Bless them, there was a 'Lizzy' awaiting me. Their ground crew started me up as I felt my way round the controls. Explaining only that as I had not flown these for some time, could I possibly borrow an instruction book. Without question this was produced and I strapped it to my knee. Quickly taxiing back to 276 dispersal I loaded Susan into the back cockpit, an operation which everyone enjoyed, as we had no ladder and the back cockpit was high and difficult to get into.

The Lysander had a peculiarity in that the trim, or balance, for take off was crucial. Too much nose down and it would not lift off, too much nose up took some effort on the control column to hold the nose down. The take off was remarkable to say the least. Eighty minutes later we landed at Portreath and got Susan out, once again to the great enjoyment of the gathered males.

She was ashen faced and shaking. I knew she had been trying to attract my attention for a lot of the journey but had given up when I found the intercom u/s. It appeared an air pressure gauge in the rear cockpit, clearly marked 'Not To Exceed 60 lbs' had slowly risen to 75 and on to 100. She had tried everything except climbing out on the wheel strut to warn me and all to no avail. When the indicator needle trembled on 120lbs, she removed her WAAF cap and covered the instrument. I was obviously happy, all my gauges had looked correct, or maybe, I had not yet reached that part of the instruction book.

My memories of the Lysander however are very pleasant. It was one of the nicest aircraft to fly. The visibility was marvellous, a bit like driving a Ford Transit Van.

All the Sea Rescue squadrons were on topline. The air war in Europe was being intensified and great formations of US Fortresses by day and British bombers by night were pounding France and Germany.

Every flight over the sea with a damaged aircraft could be a ticket to a watery grave. One of our aircraft ditched ten miles

North of Sept Isles, France, on the 7th June. We were kept constantly on the alert. Two more of our Spitfires from Harrowbeer were 'jumped' by FW 190's over the channel. One got back. AQJ P8674 Africander was shot down. The replacement aircraft 'J' was also unlucky. Sometime later I flew it often and hated it. The last I saw of that particular aeroplane was sitting forlornly at Northolt after it had attempted one last shot at trying to dispose of me into the Gasworks at Kew Bridge.

It would appear that aircraft bearing the letters AQJ were not particularly lucky for 276 Squadron pilots as the original AQJ P8674 Africander which I mention as being shot down, was at that unfortunate time being flown by Sgt Taffy Dorman when searching for a 412 Squadron RCAF pilot F/O Thatcher who on this occasion was ultimately rescued but later lost his life when he collided with another Spitfire carrying out a bombing mission a year later.

Victor Dorman together with F/O Barry Hill had the misfortune to tangle with 6 FW 190s flying out of Cherbourg and Oberlieutenant Friedrich May, an ace with 27 previous victories to his credit and now flying with 3 Staffel Jadeschwader 2. A Spitfire II was no match for the FW 190 and Taffy ended up in the drink and lucky to be alive. His story told years later makes interesting reading.

He was 'Standing in' for a chum who had lined up a promising looking date in Plymouth, Vic was a bit shattered to hear the klaxon horn blaring about 6pm. With F/O Barry Hill leading, they were soon on their way towards the Channel Islands, where half an hour later they spotted F/O Thatcher ensconced in a dinghy. At the time they thought the 'find' to be a Polish airman the squadron had been searching for earlier, so in high spirits, as per the usual drill Barry Hill assigned Taffy to circle the dinghy whilst he climbed a couple of thousand feet to transmit for a 'fix'. Some minutes later, Taffy, knowing he was short of fuel had just turned for home when he saw what he thought to be six Spitfires closing in on him from the North. A closer look however proved them to be FW190s, and he did not feel too good about that. Pushing the throttle through the gate, he emulated the Nick Berryman manoeuvre of dodging the wave tops at a great rate of knots towards a warm bed.

The FWs however took turns at knocking small chunks off his airplane, until the final straw was a cannon shell, just over his head, which smashed the gunsight and set fire to the fuel tank up front. As the flames started to lick back at him, he cut the throttle, downed flaps and splashed the Spit into the sea. The airplane sank like a stone. He was about twenty feet under the water when he managed to clear the cockpit and struggle to the surface, where he released his parachute and dinghy just remembering the latter before it floated out of his reach. He had somehow lost his helmet and boots but was relieved to find that his Mae West inflated normally. Then he managed to inflate the dinghy and get into it. It was about 7pm, the sea was calm and 'by jingo' a lot had happened in the last hour.

Nothing else was to be seen either on sea or in sky. So confident was he in our Number 276 Squadron that he thought he would be picked up within another hour. That envisaged hour turned out to be the following Sunday Week, Seven days later.

Somehow or other the survival pack from his aircraft was near him, and he knows to this day that he could never have survived without it.

After seven days of seeing 'Sweet Fanny Adams' except a Puffin he christened 'Charlie', two ME109s swooped low over him and gave him a wave.

An hour later a Dornier flying boat arrived and the pilot made such a bloody awful mess of the landing he damaged the aircraft. British and German together then had to wait patiently for the arrival of a tug, the driver of which was able to give Taffy a drink of water, which he badly needed. They all duly arrived at Greve De Leq on the North coast of Jersey on the 13th June. Two days later the Dornier crew took off only to turn the thing over and end up in hospital with broken arms and legs.

Perhaps they should have emulated 276 Squadron and put plenty of practice in at rough sea landings.

Taffy was released from hospital and set to Fresnes Gestapo Prison Hospital near Paris, where he assured me that three days in there would cure any football hooligan. Two weeks of concentrated interrogation followed, and a transfer to Stalag 6 and back to Muhlberg on Elbe where he spent nearly two years contemplating his navel, until the Russian Cavalry rode into Stalag 4B. He then had just as difficult a time escaping from them, as he had already endeavoured to escape the Germans, but a bit of 'Welsh know how' finally got him across the Elbe to join the Americans and thankfully home to England.

As for Barry Hill, the Section Leader on June 7th 1943, Barry too, high-tailed it back to Harrowbeer, where he related his story; only to perish himself in a similar incident six months later.

THE GARAGE WITH THE LEAKY ROOF

The hot summer days were a joy and when free to do so the aircrew would sprawl on the grass in the sun. The Canadians were avid poker players and taught me well, a good grounding for the business life I was later to have.

Occasional correspondence with Ray McNair 'On Your Tail' Taylor kept me informed of his well-being, if that is the right word to use, as he had endured the loss of a colleague on 197 Squadron, acted as Accompanying Officer at the burial in Lincoln, suffered a flying accident himself and spent three months in hospital.

Now, doing a ground job at Drem, he had fallen in love and was recovered sufficiently to marry the widow of the friend he had so recently buried.

The wedding was to be August 24th and I was asked to be Best Man. I was flying on the 23rd and was obviously still well lit up by a hairy rescue attempt in the Walrus on the 22nd when I failed to win a battle with the elements and taxied 20 miles in the wake of a cargo ship to the safety of Poole Harbour.

It was a fine wedding in London and I thought his bride was 'a bit of all right'. We would meet again, but meanwhile I returned to fly on the 25th.

Paul Mercer came on the scene again. Finished with 55 OTU, he joined 263 and their 'Whirlybirds'. It was nice to see Paul. We chatted over old times and it was fixed that he had the room next to mine in the new Mess, which was at crossroads on the Bere Regis to Weymouth road and adjoining the airfield.

The Whirlwinds were doing day and night intruder operations into France and were busy. Mother, Father and Alan came down for a late summer break and I booked them into an Hotel at Osmington Mill. I took all the aircrew to meet them in the evenings and they were constantly reminded of our near presence, as the Spits would roar overhead with a roll or a wing-waggle.

Alan had brought his Army Cadet uniform and, with his sergeants stripes, he easily passed as an enlisted soldier. A S/Ldr Heaton Armstrong who was the 'Chester Herald' wished to see the squadron at work as he was authorising our new squadron crest. I took him up in a Walrus and got Alan aboard. We only did a couple of sea landings in Poole Harbour but he enjoyed it and I was very proud to have piloted my brother. The date was September 17th.

Before the family returned to Ealing, Father handed me the keys of his Standard 9. It was mine for the duration of war. Having seen my performance on the BSA I suspect he thought I stood more chance of killing myself on it than in a Spitfire.

Having a car was a great advantage. Some evenings I could get into Weymouth with the boys for a beer, which was not easy on the Station as Sergeants were Sergeants, Officers were Officers and only on gala occasions did we meet in each other's messes.

Petrol shortage was a problem, but a trip in the Tiger Moth, a slight adjustment to flying time and a rubber tube usually put that right.

The Mess threw a Summer Ball or an excuse for one and the Squadrons on the station were Stood Down (relieved of operational duty) for twelve hours. I was a bit browned off because Susan could not get to it. It had been a long time since I had seen her and I felt lonely and cheated.

The night of the party I attached myself to Janet, a WAAF Catering Officer. Janet was not particularly pleased, especially as I started to drown my sorrows in drink. Several times she tried to unload me to bed but, as she dare not be seen going to my room (a bit different from today's standards), she never actually got me to bed.

Every time I was despatched, I re-appeared and each time a little more inebriated. Finally she took me to the Standard 9 and covering me up with a rug told me to have a sleep. After midnight I re-appeared to find her leaving the Mess on her cycle for her bed. It was raining and despite protests I got her to the car. I was insistent that she must not get wet. We arrived at Thatched Cottage a mile away towards Moreton.

The cottage was the WAAF Officers' Mess. Threatened with death if I made a sound and awoke her seniors, I took her to the door and safety. She congratulated me upon my decorum. Returning to the car I backed from the side road into the main Weymouth Road and put the car in first gear to move off forwards. Nothing happened. The engine revved as I let in the clutch but no movement. My confused mind thought about the engineering theories I had learned. Broken half shaft? Stripped gear box shaft? Worn clutch? Inspection at the rear found me looking at the two rear wheels lifted clear of the ground. The sturdy rear bumper had ridden straight up the sloping steel support of an invasion defensive tank trap.

I pushed, I shoved, I fell in the mud, but I could not get the darned car onto the road again. All the time it rained. I cast discretion to the winds and went back to 'The Waafery' and banged on the door loud enough to waken the dead.

I thought I had indeed, as all the 'old birds' tottered out in their curlers and dressing gowns to rock me off the tank trap. With revving engine and shouts of appreciation, I weaved my way into the night.

Arriving at the gate to the Mess garages, I had three shots at getting through it before the wind blew it shut each time and was disappointed to leave my car in a garage with a leaky roof.

The next morning I was awakened by a disapproving Jeanie with a cup of tea.

"Och ye shud be ashamed of yerself," she said. "Ha ya seen yur troosers?" I gathered from the tone of the conversation that my 'troosers' would not bear inspection, so I ignored the question. "And," she went on, pointing to the window, "just look at your car."

My eyes followed her indicating finger. Fifty yards away in the garden outside, stood the car. My room window was wide open, it was still raining and the window sill was covered in mud. I suppose it had been the quickest way in from the garage with the leaky roof! To make things even worse, Janet refused to speak to me for a week.

YOOHOO DUCKY!

The next moon period brought the Whirlwind boys the conditions they really like. Across the Channel low, through the French Coast defences and on to a target. Bomb, strafe and out. Their morale was high and their faces showed it.

On the perimeter track alongside the Crossways to Stafford Road one evening I spotted HEQ taxiing for take off. The aircraft moved slowly, outlined by the night sky, her twin Peregrine engines crackling and barking, throwing out fingers of flame into the darkness.

'Queenie' was Paul Mercer's aircraft, and I was alongside as he stopped to carry out a pre-take off check. I stepped up to the wing, took hold of the elevator and gave it a waggle. Paul felt the stick jerk in his hand and turned towards me. With an oxygen mask covering his lower face, only his eyes showed recognition and he raised a gloved hand to give me a thumbs up. Then with a staccato burst of engine that sent the dew capped grasses toppling backwards, and a crackle as he throttled back again, he swung into wind and was gone. The glow of the exhausts finally disappearing into the darkness.

I slept badly that night, and I was glad to hear the engines of four Whirlwinds return two hours later as I had seen four go off.

The next morning I heard Paul stirring next door as I hurried to breakfast and flying. Whilst at lunch I was told to return to flights quickly; a Whirlwind had been shot down over Cherbourg and was seen to crash into the sea. I should never again give Paul a thumbs up before he climbed towards the clouds.

The date was 24th October 1943. A bad day for the fighter bombers. A German cargo ship, The Munsterland, carrying Wolfram from the Far East was nearing the Atlantic shores of France. Wolfram was vital to the German steel industry as its addition to steel was part of the Tungsten hardening process, vital for bearings. Attacked repeatedly across the Bay of Biscay The Munsterland had survived and looked certain to make an arrival in Cherbourg. It was then Winston Churchill, the Prime Minister, stepped in and ordered its destruction at all costs. Twenty-four aircraft, Typhoons and Whirlwinds were despatched to do the job. Only Fourteen returned and Paul was among the missing.

So decimated was 263 Squadron by this action the Whirlwinds, of which there were only two squadrons, were replaced by Typhoons. The Commanding Officer, S/Ldr Geoff Warnes, survived the disastrous Munsterland attack only to be forced to bail out of his Tiffy over the Channel. Returning from a sweep over France, Warnes suffered engine failure whilst in the company of three other Typhoons. Faced with the choice of bailing out or ditching he chose the latter course. He must have been pretty low over the sea, as Typhoon pilots were well aware that the large radiator beneath the aircraft acted as a water scoop, the resulting ditching exercise was likely to end in a nose dive to the depths.

Warnes would have been aware of this but ditch he did and apparently escaped the cockpit. One of the Squadron pilots, an Australian by the name of Tuff, saw that his well liked leader was in the water and in trouble, sea conditions were poor. An excellent swimmer like many Australians he turned back and baled out alongside his 'boss' in order to help. Both men were lost as was another pilot P/O Hunter who stayed to circle the spot but had disappeared before the rescue boats arrived after being alerted by the fourth Typhoon who returned to base, sending w/t messages as he progressed.

Was this an action deserving of a Victoria Cross or an admonishment? In the outcome neither action transpired, but the event is still the subject of conjecture amongst now ageing Typhoon pilots. Circumstances such as these served to uncomfortably remind single engined pilots of their vulnerability.

In the closing days of October, with the summer gone and the onset of winter imminent, Fighter Command made changes to prepare for the invasion of Europe, and I found myself established at Portreath.

This suited me well, as I was able to see Susan everyday and we cemented our friendship. The month prior to my move I attained the great age of 21 years, and Sue had given me a pair of gold cufflinks suitably engraved with my initials. On the plain side was engraved the word 'MIZPAH', the translation meaning 'God be between me and thee whilst we are apart'.

Susan was a religious girl, and on one of my clandestine visits to her room in the WAAF mess at Yartrees Cottage, I was touched to see my photograph in a frame beneath which were the words of Psalm 139, Verses 8 and 9.

> *'If I take the wings of the morning*
> *and remain in the uttermost parts of the sea,*
> *Even there also shall thy hand lead me*
> *and thy right hand shall hold me.'*

Anyone visiting the RAF Memorial at Runnymede and looking towards the banks of the River Thames, across the land where the Magna Carta was signed, will find themselves reading those same words etched into the beautiful Memorial Window.

Our friendship was pure and honest, and I am sure her prayers for my safety were answered. Of course, a love affair between an Ops Officer and an Operational Pilot had some disadvantages, one of these being that when on duty she knew where and what I was flying. Sue never tried to hide her feelings, and I was a bit embarrassed one morning when leading a section of Spitfires. I skimmed over the perimeter tracks, engines high-revving and brakes burning hot, to be instructed over the R/T 'Lucas Red Leader, Scramble and Steer 220 Degrees. Be Careful.' I acknowledged with the usual 'Roger, out' but at the same time I heard another quick transmission from a 'wag' somewhere, and it was 'Oh Yoohoo Ducky.'

One evening I visited Susan's room rather longer than accepted moral standards allowed, and deciding it was advisable to avoid WAAF senior officers in the main Mess, I opened a window. Sitting astride the sill ready to jump to the ground, found myself looking down at a WAAF Squadron Officer, who enquired politely as to whether I was going in or coming out. Needless to say I was rendered speechless.

The Flight Commander at Portreath was Flight Lieutenant Dimbleby. 'Dim' was an experienced officer and used his aircrew sensibly. He was also a good drinker and party-goer and I expect he was already in training for his post-war job as Mine Host at the Bowling Green Hotel, Leicester and the Red Lion at Rothley.

He always had the well-being of the Mess at heart, and nearing Christmas I was sent on an urgent mission to St Mary's on the Isles of Scilly. I popped the Walrus down in the Bay and was looking for a mooring buoy when a man in a rowing boat came alongside and offered a two foot square package as ballast. I knew by instinct that the box contained twelve bottles of Scotch and that the urgent part of the mission was to transport it safely to the mainland, where it was in short supply.

For most of the time I was flying the Spitfire however, but acting as an instructor for rough sea landings. We had one Walrus pilot, Tiny Martin, a solicitor turned war-time aircrew, who was very inexperienced in rough water, so I took him down to St Ives Bay for a long practice session followed by an operational sortie during which he improved no end. This was fortunate for Tiny as the next day he was scrambled to find a pilot seen in a dinghy by operating Beaufighters.

Tiny took off late afternoon, found the pilot who would not have survived another night, misjudged his landing in the rough water and near darkness, smashed his tailplane, picked the pilot up, taxied through a mine field and ran the Walrus on to a Cornish beach early next morning. He was given an immediate award of the DFC. We had a great party and he was a great chap, later to become Recorder of Brighton, Sussex.

FOND FAREWELLS

I learned that soon I could expect a posting to Italy, where our troops were advancing rapidly, and the Allies were savouring success again after vanquishing the Germans in North Africa.

In the first days of January 1944 I flew my last operations for 276 Squadron, one of which gave me great satisfaction when Sgt Scott and I located a colleague, F/O Pressland from Harrowbeer, who had baled out into the Atlantic whilst flying a Typhoon with 193 Squadron.

With no time to scramble the Walrus, we guided a Naval Corvette to his rescue. Such moments were highly rewarding in a job that could sometimes be tedious.

Saying farewell to Susan was the worst part of leaving Portreath and the rocky beaches of Cornwall, but five days leave in London helped to mend a broken heart.

Setting off early one morning from Redruth, I drove the Standard 9 Saloon as I had been advised by my father. He counselled that at 30mph the car would last me a lifetime, any faster would prove expensive. I had little money saved in the bank, so the journey took me nine hours. The last two fatiguing hours were driven with little forward visibility due to the dim headlights imposed by the wartime lighting restrictions.

Some signposts had re-appeared now that the threat of invasion was passed, but long journeys by road in those days were only for the adventurous. I knew that my leave this time would be difficult as far as my Mother's feelings were concerned. The war and the bombing raids of the past four years had without doubt left their mark on her. On the surface she was her usual cheerful self, but the thought of husband and sons in danger was a constant worry, as it was to most family women.

The nightly raids on London still persisted and to the average family there was little to laugh about. Food rationing was very stringent and it must have been difficult to conjure up the odd little treat for a special occasion, especially as Father was a man who, like his Mother before him, expected the very best and found it difficult to understand the word ration.

Just prior to the war I often saw a 40lb York ham delivered by a grateful customer and cases of spirits, wine and cigars would arrive as gifts to him each Christmas. Five thousand cigarettes in total was quite normal. Bank Managers were held in esteem and customers showed their appreciation. Now it had all changed and six ounces of bacon would last a family for a week.

Mother was doing her bit for the war effort serving with a WVS mobile canteen, and had taken a part-time job with a Chelsea solicitor. Alan was approaching his last year at school, and could not wait to finish in order that he could enlist in the Army.

All my old friends had dispersed and were involved in the War somewhere. Nevertheless it was a happy homecoming and the rounds of family farewells began.

Some of my younger cousins had grown up, and I got a kick out of taking Uncle Stanley's elder daughter, Eileen, to a dance at the Hammersmith Palais where we danced to the early hours of the morning. She has told me since that she was terribly proud of being escorted by a Royal Air Force Pilot.

My Father was secretly pleased to get his beloved car back again, especially as I was able to hand over some extra petrol coupons with it. Leave usually entitled servicemen to extra petrol, otherwise the normal ration was about 3 gallons a month. I was aware that the final day of leave and 'Au Revoir' would be tearful, as behind brave faces each one of us knew it might be the last. In consequence I misled my parents into thinking that I was to report to Morecombe a day earlier than in fact I did.

My original plan was to spend the last day and night at the YMCA Tottenham Court Road, where I still had a few contacts from the concert party days, and which was only a stone's throw from St Pancras Station. I had talked over the telephone to Betty, the joint girlfriend of Frank Ellis and myself, and who was still at Amersham Hospital.

Arriving at the YMCA, I must say I was delighted to see her, and we resolved to have a farewell party to end all parties. It did not work out that way however, as we could find no friends to join us, so undeterred we made it a party for two.

Thirty-six hours lay between our meeting and farewell, and we started to paint the town red. Betty and I had known each other for over four years, knew each other's families, had experienced snatched holidays together early in the war with the YWCA and YMCA, we had danced, swum, played tennis and ice-skated. We had loved and quarrelled and over the four years I had considered her both girlfriend and sister alternately, but this time was different.

Like the song from Gigi, those flashing eyes sent me crashing through the ceiling. We danced at the Palais and the Astoria, we dined at the Strand Palace and we attended a show at the London Palladium. This proved to be very embarrassing when during a dance routine to the popular tune of the day "He Wears a Pair of Silver Wings", I, together with other pilots of all nationalities were whisked out of our stall seats by those glorious Tiller girls.

They got the rabble into a chorus line with them, the music changed tempo and there was I with what seemed to be half the population of London looking on high kicking and tapping my troubles away.

In retrospect, we made a good job of the routine, as all being young and conditioned to drill, our timing was spot on. I was just hoping somebody would not be saying to my Father, 'Saw your son on stage at the London Palladium last night.' To cap it all, I walked into Arthur Jarvis, my Bank Manager, the next morning. I introduced him to Betty and my eyes told him to keep mum.

It was all over, a wave and a tear at St Pancras Station, and I was on my way to Morecombe. At least I would be able to hold an intelligent conversation with more experienced men should I ever enter the Pearly Gates of Heaven.

Morecombe was a holding unit only, so it was only necessary to update on inoculations which once again were done on the mass production line – and by the time the thirtieth man was due for a jab, the needle was pretty blunt.

New faces and new friends to be made and without doubt birds of a feather flock together, and it was good to meet up with P/O Egerton-Green, the keep fit fanatic from Harrowbeer, who spent his spare moments leaping about in the cold without a shirt, whilst the less stalwart huddled round a stove with a hand of cards. As experienced pilots we would be travelling to many different parts of the World. For me I knew it was Italy. A service-man leaving his native shores for the unknown has very strong feelings for family and country.

Out for a meal with the boys one evening I found myself in The Tivoli Cafe, Morecombe. On the back of the menu card was printed some prose. Those words I tore off and took overseas with me. They read:

ENGLAND
I love England for its physical and spiritual tranquillity because it has no scented gardens or wandering fakirs, or terrorist Llamas, none of the elements that create them. No Goblins more malicious than Puck, a land where there is little cruelty and violence, and less unkindness than elsewhere.

Not one serviceman in that Cafe on that night would have disagreed with those sentiments, and with that in mind they went away to defend those things they loved.

Transit camps were always a bore, and this one was no exception but after only a few days I was travelling to Liverpool and boarding the RMS Stirling Castle. For an officer, troopship accommodation was much improved and 6 to a cabin normally holding 4 was luxury. The U Boat menace was still very much a problem, but we nosed out into the Irish Sea and became part of a convoy, with the Catalinas and Sunderlands of Coastal Command overhead and much in evidence.

However, it was to be a pleasant trip and almost a holiday atmosphere pervaded the ship, helped by the fact that aboard we carried a load of entertainers for the overseas troops.

The Merry Widow Company, from the West End, Sadlers Wells Ballet, some ENSA, Geraldo and his Band were either there or represented. Many officers were allocated responsibilities, mine being Officer in Charge of all this lot.

My task was to see that they had no administration problems as far as accommodation was concerned, to take charge on 'boat stations' drill and to keep them below decks after 10pm.

It may sound easy, but a more undisciplined bunch I had yet to meet. To most of the men I was a joke, and the women played me up as only a woman can. The ballet girls always had their life preserver tapes incorrectly tied, and correcting this often required close body contact. After a few days I decided to give up the unequal struggle and settle down to enjoy it.

The Army Officer on the Boat Station next to me was the OC WRNS, and he had very little trouble. I thought for a couple of days that the one pip on his shoulder was that of a subaltern, and I pulled his leg considerably. I just called him Inchcape. 'Come on, jump about Inchcape' I would say. 'Bloody Army late on parade again.' Then I discovered that the one pip was a crown, that he was a Major and a Lord and his family owned the ship we were sailing on. I somewhat modified my form of greeting from then on.

Four days sailing brought us into Gibraltar and the Mediterranean, warm winter sunshine, porpoises riding along with the swell of the ship and moonlit nights.

On one such night I caught sight of 'Georgina', Geraldo's singer, on deck after the mandatory below-decks time. I knew it was Georgina by her flowing golden locks hanging down her back. She was looking out to sea and completely oblivious of my presence. It was my responsibility to see that she obeyed the rules.

Approaching her from behind, I gave her a cheeky slap on the bottom and said, 'Come on old girl, off to bed.' I was a bit mortified as Georgina swung round. 'I beg your pardon', a mature WREN officer in shirt and skirt enquired. Trying to explain that I always treated Georgina 'that way' only got me deeper into the 'cacky' and I retired in considerable confusion.

After a few more days at sea, and another ship's concert, we nosed into a foreign dock. The deck workers wore galabiyas and fezzes, and a large advertisement proclaimed, "Haig Whisky Welcomes You to Port Said".

'Hells, Bells', I thought, 'this isn't Italy, it's bloody Egypt'. And it was.

A PACK OF WOLVES

Almaza, near Cairo, was a tented encampment and a week there nearly drove me to drink. I found RAF HQ Middle East and stirred a Wing Commander to sufficient motivation and annoyance to have me moved. I found myself standing in the rear of an open truck bouncing and swaying up the desert road which leads from Alexandria for the whole length of the North African Coast.

Egypt in February can be very cold and that particular morning it was. In half an hour I, straight from England and complete with greatcoat and gloves, was frozen. It was then that I noticed an Australian Pilot Officer Air Gunner without any such protection, looking as blue as his dark blue uniform and trying to hang on to the front guard rail of the truck. Seeing that his hand was numb with cold, I stuck my hand in a pocket and offered him the use of a glove.

From then on, he used always to introduce me to his Aussie friends as "the first decent Pommie bastard" he had yet to come across. The gunner was Bill Dransfield from Bondi Beach, NSW, and we were both bound for LG91 Amaryia and 294 Squadron.

Bill had been up and down the desert for a year seeing service with Marauders and helping to drive the Germans back to Tripoli. Here they found themselves pincered between British troops advancing West and the Americans advancing East and decided to evacuate to Sicily and Italy.

For them it was the beginning of the end, as their Russian front was also crumbling. There was a lot of fighting to do yet however, and it was to be sixteen months before the Germans laid down arms and twenty months before the Japanese surrendered.

Whilst the assault troops of the three services battled it out in the front line, the back up troops and training squadrons were left in the rear. For Bill and me at Amaryia it was to be a quiet time. 294 Squadron commanded by Wing Commander R G Walker DFC was part of Middle East Coastal Command and was equipped with Wellingtons and Walrus aircraft used for search and recovery, taking in the desert as well as the sea.

Upon arrival, I accepted the inevitable. I was type cast as a Walrus ASR pilot. Both new to the squadron, Bill and I had no difficulty in becoming crewed up and were later joined by another Flying Officer Harry Gibbins, newly arrived from the Seychelle Islands in the Indian Ocean, where he had done a tour with a Catalina squadron.

I was fortunate, as they were both to prove excellent airmen and companions. Bill and I were of similar temperament, while 'Gibby' was rather more reserved and cautious. From one or two bits of correspondence of that time, I have gleaned that he was not always too happy about the way Bill and I set about the job, but seemed resigned to the fact that I was a reasonable enough pilot who was aiming to see the war through.

As for Bill, he was a 'tough cookie' and would have gone through hell and high water with me, all based on the fact that I had loaned him a glove and was his idea of an English gentleman.

Living in the desert was a new experience for me, but not too unenjoyable once the first shock of primitive living was over. Food was not enjoyable and hot meat loaf, Spam and dehydrated vegetables were the staple diet. When water was plentiful, one could take a shower from a forty gallon oil drum propped above head height. The latrines were poles over a pit where one pole sufficed for five men. The desert here was very stony, not the loose sand so often seen in films about the French Foreign Legion.

Two other squadrons used the landing ground, No. 6 with their Hurricanes and the 13th Hellenic Squadron flying Marylands. Part of the flying operational risk seemed to be dodging the Marylands and their Greek crews on take off. They always appeared to dislike the direction most other people decided upon, but they were never dull. When things went very quiet they could be relied upon to disappear temporarily into the depths of sea or desert, which of course was very good for keeping 294 on the alert. With the occasional search and sea landing practice, we kept our hands in.

Bill had never even seen a seaplane before and Gibby was used only to the large Catalinas. The first few trips we did, landing and taking off from the sea in the bone shaking cavorting Walrus, were an eye opener to both of them. More than once I saw Gibby turn deathly pale whilst Bill cursed his luck trying to get some sense out of the TR9 radio. This was while sea water could be pouring in through the open hatch of the cockpit as we made a particularly difficult take off. As I used to explain, at least the Mediterranean was warm, and they should have experienced the cold Atlantic to qualify for a moan.

In this manner we got over the first couple of months. As a crew we settled down well, but it did seem strange to me to have to consider other people and even to take the advice of a Navigator. Until then, it had been up to me to relocate myself when lost. I had to admit however, that when searching for long hours at sea the operation was more likely to be of some accuracy when Gibby had his chart and pencil to hand. The rivalry between us was always evident and I was constantly reminding him that to me a 'Nav' was just extra weight.

Alexandria was the nearest point of civilisation and occasionally we got a day and a night away. The Hotel Mediterranee was our favourite stop. Some of the WRNS girls I had met on the boat were stationed in Alexandria and if we could give them sufficient warning they would get evenings off to be with us. I was most amused to see, when visiting the 'Wrenery' an alphabetical list of names – all male, with comments alongside.

The main comments appeared to be:

'Wolf'

'Wolf in Sheep's clothing'

'Sheep in Wolf's clothing'

'Sheep in Sheep's clothing'

'Wolf in Wolf's clothing'.

I was never able to return to see which category I fitted into but from what I can remember I cannot think of an occasion when any of them would have had much to comment about. 'Ineffectual' might just have appeared, whereas Bill Dransfield would have been listed as "Dransfield, Bill, F/O, Australian – Wolf in Wolf's clothing, Keep yours On.'

THE GODFATHER

I was corresponding regularly with Ray McNair-Taylor and his wife Sherry. I knew that he was grounded still and that he felt deeply about not being in the air. My letters to him were of an encouraging nature, always talking of when it was all over and the great fortune they shared with an impending child. As early as March 13th I wrote 'I bet 10 shillings it will be a boy with black hair and Harry-Roy-eyes' (large eyes) 'and his first words will be "Dadda, I'm on your tail"'. How prophetic can one get?

In the April, the squadron base removed to Edku just south of Aboukir and in the May I, with team, was quickly sent to Gambut to take over from a crew who had come to a sticky end in the Tobruk area. The dead pilot's name was Jack Martin from Newcastle and I had the unpleasant task of packing his personal effects off to his wife. Amongst his flying kit was a superb pair of all leather 'Escape' boots. So named because the tops could be cut off, leaving a normal pair of black shoes which would be less noticeable in enemy occupied territory. Being government property I changed these with my own less prestigious boots and wore them for many years during and after the war.

Gambut, for the Walrus, was over three hours flying from base, so we were quite cut off and living conditions were very basic. There I was kept busy, searching mostly for twin-engined bomber aircraft of the Marauder, Beaufighter and Mosquito type which failed to return after bombing the enemy in the Aegean and Adriatic areas. One such mission involved the picking up of four German aircrew, one of whom was so belligerent that I was delighted to hand them over to a Royal Naval Gunboat. Bill was in his element, giving as good as he took, but the situation was potentially dangerous and Gibby and I were not feeling heroic.

Returning to the Coast we had an engine failure and had to be rescued ourselves by an RAF Rescue Launch from Derna. It was a long day, for when we arrived in Derna Harbour we had been at sea for six hours.

Bill repaid his debt to the launch skipper by offering to rid the bilges of rats. Using one of our smoke floats, he pulled the pin forgetting there was no smoke without fire. The joint efforts of my crew and the launch crew saved the day however, and a bit of paint here and there hid a multitude of sins.

The engine repair to the Walrus took four days and was carried out by an earnest bunch of engine fitters from Gambut who, unused to tossing about, kept dropping their spanners into the water. Bill came into his own again as he was a magnificent swimmer and diver, so consequently much of the stuff was retrieved.

The story went at the time that the engineering officer in charge obtained the engine piston and cylinder he required from an Italian aircraft which had crashed in the desert behind Derna. Until now I have never been sufficiently interested to find out if some Italian aircraft did use Bristol Pegasus engines however I am informed that the SM79 did. Before 1939 Bristol did make engines for other countries, so there could be a foundation for the tale.

Then the three of us got sand fly fever. This illness causes stomach pains and constant visits to the lavatory. After an air test which proved to be satisfactory, we wanted to get back to Gambut, over an hour and a half flying time to the East. A joint visit to an Army Doctor filled us sufficiently with stomach cement to enable me to contemplate the trip.

A bouncy sea take off did not help matters and I soon noticed Gibby's gradually tightening lips. The occasional bellow from Bill at the back urging me to "Open up the bleedin' taps mate" alerted me to a degree of urgency to shorten the air time as much as possible. By the time I could see the airfield dust at Gambut, forty miles and twenty minutes away, Gibby's legs were tread-milling. Bill's shouts were replaced by his appearance at my right shoulder and looking very red in the face. I myself was feeling uneasy.

When the airfield was reached, I told the Airfield Control I had an emergency and was coming straight in. I heard them advise other aircraft to clear the runway and landed the Walrus. I literally flew it in the direction of the lavatory which I knew to be a 'three holer'.

By the time I had knocked the switches off, Bill and Gibby were running, knees bent, for the last thirty yards. Taking a deep breath, I too hopped over the side but forgot to unplug the microphone which was attached to my flying helmet, so spent several seconds untangling myself (which nearly proved disastrous). I arrived at the tin hut to find holes one and two occupied by gently smiling Bill and Gibby. The third was occupied by someone else. This was no time for niceties so I went round the back.

Later that day Flying Control rang the flight to ask what the emergency was. Someone informed them, "The crew had the shits". We wondered how that would be worded in the Operations Book.

The Walrus repair was not permanent, it reappeared and three days later we were relieved by another aircraft and crew and we flew back to Edku.

Shortly before leaving Gambut I was to write to Ray and Sherry complaining that I had received no word from them for six or seven weeks, that a child could not be taking up all their time yet and would they write to me when the baby was born. My news was that I was finding it difficult to keep my clothing clean and was going through many bars of Swan Soap. I could heat water in an open-topped five-gallon drum which, placed upon a mound of petrol-soaked sand, soon brought the water to boil. Wash day was fraught with peril, as my singed arms and eyebrows showed to the full.

Back in the Delta and with less opportunity to hog the flying hours, I set about making myself as comfortable as I could. I started by lowering the floor of my tent to give more headroom and borrowed a quilted aircraft engine cover from maintenance flight. The effect was pleasing, I had wall to wall carpeting. Two strategically placed five-gallon drums gave hot and cold running water. The hot in the evening only, as 'Mr Sun' did the heating.

Living with Bill was not easy in a confined space, so I contrived to get him moved to a tent with another untidy chap. Gibby made his own arrangements too. Sometimes I was sharing with an eccentric Canadian Wellington pilot who was as nutty as a fruit cake, but after I discovered two ducks named Malesh and Alekefik swimming in my sunken bath area, he too was banished. I reigned in solitary state surrounded by my own contrived luxury. Outside the tent stood some date palms and beyond them was the bay and swimming. I had it made.

June 6th dawned and I was ordered to find and pick up something reported in a shipping lane West of Alexandria. It took three hours and twenty minutes to locate the object, a floating mine. Thinking it best not to pick it up, I told Bill to blow it up with the Lewis gun. The combination of my piloting and his gunnery turned that little job into a debacle, but we did sink it. Meanwhile on the North coast of France, the Allied invasion had begun which made our contribution to the war effort appear pretty feeble. The crew grabbed a week's leave and we purchased the other half of the Hotel Mediterranee in Alex.

It was the holiday I needed. In retrospect the past eighteen months had been hard going. The weather was lovely, the WRNS

By the time I had knocked the switches off, Bill and Gibby were running, knees bent, for the last thirty yards. Taking a deep breath, I too hopped over the side but forgot to unplug the microphone which was attached to my flying helmet, so spent several seconds untangling myself (which nearly proved disastrous). I arrived at the tin hut to find holes one and two occupied by gently smiling Bill and Gibby. The third was occupied by someone else. This was no time for niceties so I went round the back.

were willing and I heard that on June 20th David Raymund McNair-Taylor had been born to an overjoyed Ray and Sherry. I was to be his Godfather.

The war news was encouraging and the World Service BBC News was listened to regularly to hear how the Allied landing in France was progressing.

If the past year had patterned my life, the next three months were to put me on a reciprocal course to my present heading. Almost certainly the incident on April 4th, 1943, (after which I found myself being switched from fighters to flying boats) probably saved me from a lot of unpleasant happenings. By now, one year later, I would have been engaged in the invasion and the advance into Europe. The fighter and fighter-bombers were heavily committed supporting the ground troops and the losses were high. There would be no second chance of a successful invasion and the Allies threw in everything they had. Quickly breaking through the German defences was of paramount importance and support fighters were expendable.

I had heard that Charles Lawrence was with a Typhoon Squadron again after damaging an ear drum, so I thought it likely that he would be in the thick of the fighting.

On the squadron I never heard the subject voiced and I cannot remember any strong feelings myself about missing the invasion, but secretly I think we felt lucky to have missed it.

RAY MCNAIR-TAYLOR

A letter from Ray McNair-Taylor written 14th July from Netheravon confirmed three things in particular. Firstly, yes his son did have dark hair and his eyes were large, but blue. Secondly, he was expecting to return to operational flying again and he felt confident, but not to forget our agreement over Mac the spaniel. He also made a strong reference to his pleasure at my being David's Godfather and to how much my friendship meant to him.

An August 4th letter expressed anxiety in several ways. He talked of Sherry being upset and weepy when flying was discussed, even to the extent that she was weeping over my letters and worrying about my safety.

A paragraph ended with 'Oh how I am looking forward to our little reunion dinner at the Savoy, Nick. Just you, Betty, Sherry and myself, and if I can't make it, I have a son now to take my place.'

He told also of a visit he had received from Charles, whose main comment about the baby was "Deadly, isn't it". He said that this 'Typhoon war' in Normandy was Bullshit, that he had burst his recently repaired eardrum again and was off flying.

Ray concluded the letter with, 'That "tail" of yours is never out of sight. Bye bye old horse, devotedly Mac, Sherry, David and the dog.'

Letters always took a minimum of three weeks to arrive in the Middle East. I expect it was early September when I received that one, by which time Ray was settling in at 57 OTU Eshott, Northumberland, and was flying Spitfires. By the 13th September he was showing signs of nervous strain, and on the 17th at a meeting in York, where Sherry was taken by her Mother and Father, he showed definite signs of cracking up.

I have never considered myself a psychologist but I do know how young men felt in those day, and also how the RAF would have reacted at the same time. This is my opinion of the circumstances covering the period 17th to 30th September. I am speaking from first hand experience as I had quite a 'wobbly' myself, following my two accidents in 1942.

Ray was an exceedingly proud man and it would have been his wish to get into the war again, joining friends he had trained with two years earlier. Perhaps the fact that he had married the young widow of a pilot, with the added responsibility of a son, may have worried him about this ultimate welfare should he also be killed. In consequence he was torn between loyalty to family and loyalty to friends and Country.

Once a 'wobbly' starts, it is very difficult to surmount. The only hope to get over it is a combination of luck, encouragement and success. Normal will-power on its own is insufficient.

57 OTU, at that time, had an influx of newly-trained off Canadian pilots. With all due respect, Ray would not have found such company easy. Canadian pilots were almost invariably noisy, brash and pushy. I have heard it said that two on a fighter squadron was about enough and that any more was asking for a takeover.

Do not take my remarks to be offensive, as they were great chaps and it would have been a longer war without them. But in this situation the alchemy could have been wrong.

On the face of it, as a Flight Lieutenant, Ray should have run rings round them, but he could not as his confidence was not yet rebuilt. He would have found criticism hard to take. Take offs, landings and formation flying would have been particularly difficult for him.

Sometimes he would want to pack up the whole damn business, and I am sure he actually got round to talking about it to doctors and senior officers. All the time the system was dragging him on. While people were talking about his problem, his desperate hope would have been that it would all be different tomorrow.

Telephone calls to Sherry showed him to be mentally very disturbed. One doctor was stupid enough to mention 'Lack of Moral Fibre'.

'LMF' was a dirty expression in the Royal Air Force, and some aircrew happily escaped their responsibilities by admitting to it. This would not have been for Ray. Fiercely proud of his family and background, he had to carry on until he died. Which is what he did on September 30th 1944, when his aircraft dived into the sea at Drudridge Bay, Northumberland.

Four miles from the coast, he was flying in formation with others when his and another aircraft collided. The other pilot baled out and lived to tell the tale. Ray's body and aircraft were never recovered.

Amongst the names recorded at the RAF Memorial to Airmen with an Unknown Grave at Runnymede, I quite often gaze at two names in particular. For me they stand out from the other twenty thousand. They are 127883 F/O P. Mercer and 127884 F/Lt R.R. McNair-Taylor. I always feel particularly close. Perhaps it is because my Service Number was 127882.

GOING HOME

At Edku, Bill was becoming quite excited at the prospect of returning to Australia. He had completed two years in North Africa and thought he might get home before going on to a new job. 'Gibby' had been out of England for two years and he was due for a rest.

I was the overseas 'New Boy' and knowing we would shortly be split up as a crew, I visited HQME again to apply for Photographic Reconnaissance Spitfires in the Far East. This was a carefully-planned bit of skulduggery, knowing that I had been out of England for only six months. Accordingly, there was no chance of a return there and I wanted a job of my choice.

The fighter war in Europe would be tough going and after a year flying the Walrus I would need a refresher at least. Last but not least I did not fancy getting shot at from close range. Failing that, I opted for a secondment to the Fleet Air Arm, as I had seen a request for volunteers.

Bill left Edku and we exchanged addresses, hoping to meet after the war. 'Gibby' and I did another twenty trips together using any Tom, Dick or Harry gunner who would fly with us.

Bill nearly did not make it to Australia. On one of his last trips with me, returning from a lengthy sortie, he complained so much about the heat that I complied with his request for a swim and duly put the Walrus down on a calm sea. Bill was over the side in a flash and 'Gibby' threw him a Mae West as I prepared for a practice take off and landing. When the sea was calm, the Walrus used to stick to the surface of the water and one had to rock her off. Once the initial contact was broken, it was all easy.

We had a long run for the take off and I turned to make a normal pattern before landing. On the downwind leg, looking into the sun and sparkling water, I realised I could not see Bill and to make matters worse neither could 'Gibby'. A long cross-wind leg enabled me to get the sun behind us, but still no sign of Bill. I felt panic gripping my stomach as 'Gibby' advised a square search and put his navigational expertise to work. To our great relief, we spotted him in five more minutes and so relieved was I, that I swooped low over his head and dropped a smoke marker, which was shaped like a small bomb. Bill was quite oblivious to the trauma I was experiencing and was more concerned that I had nearly "knocked his bloody head off with the bleedin' marker".

Anyway, he was to get back to Australia, as we picked him up. I should have known better than to agree to Bill's cranky ideas. On another occasion he had done the same thing, inveigling me into the sea as well. 'Gibby' was left in charge of the Walrus with its engine stopped. My swimming had not improved from the days when Buster had won the cup at Maldon and it was only when the wind-swept Walrus was many yards away from me that I realised I would have a job to get back. Exhausted, I finally climbed back aboard. Bill of course with his powerful crawl had no difficulty, but just imagine the embarrassing situation should I not have made it.

As it was, nobody was to know. I gathered my promotion to Flight Lieutenant, became the odd job pilot and did some instructing of the new boys coming to replace us.

My boss expressed a desire to fly with me on my last trip with 294 squadron and he sat in the second pilot's seat. The trip was to be a 'serviceability Air and Water' test on an aircraft returned from Maintenance Unit after a major inspection, No. 3013.

With a wonderful excuse to show off a bit, I went through my repertoire like a seasoned performer on the halls. I carried out every manoeuvre a little faster than I normally would have done and held her on the water for a long time on take off. Then, with a very steep climb and full throttle, I pulled the old girl into a vertical climb.

I had never looped a Shagbat but now I would. Just before going over the top I felt someone grab my right shoulder. It was 'Gibby' shaking his head and waving one arm, the other he was holding on with. Reluctantly I let her slide over into a stall turn and we sped earthwards again to a greasy landing. That was that, September 26th and the last ever flight in the Walrus.

Sometimes in a nostalgic mood, I know that despite the ungainly, unromantic appearance, they were the most exciting of all the aircraft I ever flew.

My simpatico with them must have manifested itself in some way, as Wing Commander Walker assessed my flying ability on them as 'Above the Average'. I was pleased with that from such a squadron.

On the 30th September, the day Ray was killed, I was in Cairo expecting to go to the RAF in Burma, as the Navy would not take pilots above the rank of Flying Officer but that suited me.

Patience has never been one of my stronger virtues and the early October days just dragged. I got around to seeing some of the treasures from the Valley of the Kings and I visited the Pyramids. It all seemed such a waste of time. At long last after five years of war it seemed that victory was in sight. Every day saw an improvement on the Allied advance and I wanted to be in at the finish, not sitting on my backside at Almaza.

On the 8th October, I received an air letter from my father which brought news that shattered me. Ray had died in an air crash.

As soon as I was sufficiently composed, I penned a letter to Sherry. Two sentences I will extract from it in order that the depth of family feeling may be fully appreciated. I quote:

Ray was always more than a friend to me, I think we regarded each other as brothers, who somehow got separated at birth.

*Perhaps you will know that it was his wish that should
anything happen that he should be unable to look after you
and David, that I should see that all was well with you both.*

Your sincere friend, Nickie.

Always a good believer in fate and that life is pre-ordained, I was hardly surprised to be told by 203 Group HQ to stand by for a flight to England. It seemed that somewhere back home there was a woman, a child and a dog who needed a bit of a leg-up.

RE-UNIONS

The flight was by a DC3 Dakota and the seventeen hour journey via El Adem, Catonia and Istres to Lyneham would have been tedious but for the fact that I spent some hours as second pilot, deciding that the Flying Officer doing this job was certainly earning his 13s 6d a day.

While at Istres, I saw some of the happiness generated by the French people at their impending freedom from the oppression of the Germans and some of their own collaborators.

Upon arrival at Lyneham I kissed the soil of England, and I meant it. So glad was I to be back. I prophesied that it would take wild horses to get me abroad again. Forty three years on I have not changed my views.

It was evening when I arrived at Lyneham, and I decided to get a night's rest before proceeding to London on leave, but before going to bed I phoned Ealing 2826. The phone was answered by a voice I knew well. It was an Australian voice which greeted me with the words "Holy Cow, what in the name of hell are you doing home." I told Bill the tale and he advised me not to arrive home too quickly as he was using my bed.

Home I went, however, as soon as I could. The ensuing leave was made all that more pleasant by the fact that Bill was home too. My Mother and Father were very welcoming to him and he enjoyed English hospitality so much, he chose an Ealing girl for a wife, and married in St Mary's Church (where Cousin Ken and I had been confirmed) and returned to Australia with her.

Dear Bill, he was such a rascal. No woman or can of beer was safe in his company. He used sometimes to take bottle tops off using his teeth and his favourite toast to the ladies was

"Here's to the breezes, which lift the chemises from little girls kneeses. It pleases, it teases – Oh Jeesis, Oh Jeesis, Ooh Christ."

Certainly he injected a new slant to humour in my life, something I have never had cause to regret.

As soon as I was able, I contacted Sherry in Lincoln. It was arranged that I collected Mac the Springer from Manchester. He had been a bit of a problem for Ray with the changing of jobs and a new baby. Mac was being cared for by a friend, so I took a train to Manchester.

He was a powerful well-built animal and two years older than when he had flown an air test with me in a Hurricane back in December 1942. Mac demonstrated his uncontrolled enthusiasm by pulling me off the step of a moving bus in the centre of Manchester. Not only was it he and I in the middle of a muddy street, but also the dog basket, blanket, bowl and my suitcase.

Anxious that I should not take offence at his behaviour he then insisted on sitting on my lap for most of the journey to Lincoln, and giving me the occasional lick to show that he really did appreciate my company.

Arriving at Lincoln, it was saddening to see Sherry with her baby in such a low state. She was living with her parents and was doing some work in the family business. Her nerves were in a terrible state and she was taking sedative medicine.

There is no doubt that fortune had played Valerie (Sherry's real name) some diabolical tricks. Her brother Eric serving in the Royal Navy had been badly injured whilst serving in HMS Curacoa during the Norwegian Campaign in 1940.

She was only just seventeen when she met and fell in love with a young Frenchman, Roger Bokobza. Roger came from Marseilles where he had lived at 27 Rue Tapis Vert. Destined to follow the medical profession, war had interrupted his studies, and he had joined the French Air Force. With the German conquest of France, he had been forced to flee the country. Several of his relatives were already in labour camps.

Escaping via Algeria and Gibraltar, he had joined the Royal Air Force and was stationed at Waddington when he met Valerie and asked her to marry him. He was then sent to Saskatchewan, Canada, for flying training where he gained his wings and returned to England in June 1942. Roger completed his AFU at Watton flying Masters, did a Hurricane OTU and married Valerie on the completion of the course at St Giles' Church, Lincoln on November 14th.

197 Squadron were forming at Drem in early December and he was one of the first pilots to be attached to them. There was little flying done in the December due to shortage of aircraft. Ray McNair-Taylor then joined the squadron in January and they became friends. As more Typhoons arrived at the squadron, flying was stepped up towards attaining Operational status which they did on February 12th. Married three months to the day, on February 14th 1942, Roger flew a Typhoon into the side of a hill. Ray accompanied his body to Lincoln for burial, where he met Valerie for the first time. Ray injured himself in a flying accident three days later.

Roger's death, at the age of 20, was only one of the thousands of tragedies that befell the families of our Allies. Sometimes not aware of the sad news for many years, locked away as they were in Fortress Europe, the iron walls of which were not to be breached until June 1944; and here Valerie found herself in a position of not knowing whether her own or official efforts to impart the new of Roger's death was ever received in France.

In September 1945 however, contact was established with Roger's parents and letters and meetings took place.

By any stretch of the imagination I wonder if the generations of the intervening years could fully appreciate the heartrending emotions that were endured by parents and their sons and daughters at that time. From France, Belgium, Norway, Denmark, Poland, Czechoslovakia .... they came. Mostly in their early twenties, to England, to fight at our side for the hoped for liberation of their families and their beloved homelands – adventures and success are fruitless unless the outcome of such can be appreciated by those we love best.

In retrospect I am able to envisage Roger's short life. A loving family, happy school days with a successful climax, and then, War! Forced to flee his country, family and friends, to escape the persecution that would undoubtedly have overtaken him, as it did his father and younger brother.

He achieved his goal, to attain his wings and be given an aircraft with which to fight his way back to home again. All this with tremendous effort and willpower. Never able to tell his loved ones of his adventure and success. No meetings, no letters from home, no kiss of warmth and love, no fatherly handshake of congratulation. Just the ability to 'press on regardless' would have carried him forward.

It must have been a wonderful moment when he found someone of his own in Valerie. Now, there was again a person in his life with which to share the joys and disappointments, and not to mention the ultimate joy of holding a wife in his arms. The joy for either of them lasted not too long. Married in November 1942, Roger died three months later on St Valentine's Day, February 1943.

In 1945 Marie Bokobza, Roger's mother, wrote letters in which her years of deprivation can be felt. She writes:

When I received your letter it seemed to me it was like getting a letter from my son Roger and therefore I was so pleased. It seems to me he is still alive and I see him before me always smiling. Small things gave him great pleasure.

It took the Germans to occupy Marseilles for me to have so much hatred of them. They have caused so much misery into so many families in this war but it has brought them no satisfaction.

With the occupation of Vichy France the Bokobza family were pushed forcibly from pillar to post, harried and hounded. Monsieur Bokobza was pushed into a forced labour camp and, later with Lucien the younger son then aged seventeen and a half years, were due to be rounded up for a concentration camp when they escaped to a farm in Riole until the day of liberation.

As I write these happenings, I realise that my own war effort was of small magnitude. However, I remain proud to have been associated with similar fellows to myself, who by their individual small contributions attained ultimate victory against oppression and barbarism.

Valerie's parents were very hospitable to me and I think my visit cheered her up a little. She had been visited by 'Bullshit' Charles who had perked her up a bit, as only Charles would have known how to, and had proffered marriage if she found herself at a loss for something better to do. I was not there to witness the proposal, but I knew Charles so well I am sure that is how he said it.

I returned to Ealing after two days and introduced Mac to Father, Mother and Alan. Mac made himself at home and suffered Ginger Fur the cat with forbearance. Ginger Fur suffered with canker in his ears. Alan loved the cat and as my Father could never be expected to carry out such an objectionable job as cleaning out ears, took over as resident vet.

Ginger lived in a box, on which was beautifully painted "Ginger Fur Esquire, Ear Specialist." My brother's humour was showing signs of maturity.

ONE MAN AND HIS DOG

The Royal Air Force had not forgotten my existence and I was asked to attend a re-deployment board in North West London. The interview took up one day and the board asked my opinion of a suitable employment. I mentioned just about everything but four-engined bombers. It became obvious that my opinion was only asked for out of courtesy, as before leaving they decided that I was very suitable to carry out the only job I had not mentioned.

I was to become a Flying Instructor and would I make hence immediately to No 2 FIS (Flying Instructors School) at Montrose in Scotland.

It was fun to go North with all the trappings that I had put aside three years previously. Always restricted to baggage weight when travelling, I gave free rein to my new-found freedom from such inconvenience. I knew I should be at FIS for three months and I set forth with dog, portable radiogram, records, banjolele and some civilian clothes.

The Mess was two miles from Montrose, situated in a magnificent country house called Rosemount which had spacious grounds. Within the grounds were situated some long wooden huts, each containing about six rooms. The dog and I chose the room nearest the main door in one of these huts and made the acquaintance of the allocated batman. We decided it would be quite comfortable here. Mac and I had become firm friends by now and taken all round he was obedient. He understood service people and service ways and got on well with everyone. He certainly ruled the roost. He was the only dog there and in consequence did very well from the kitchens.

The airfield was a short coach ride away and Mac and I made the round trip twice a day. If I happened to be flying when the first bus went to lunch, Mac would sometimes get on it, demand his perks from the Mess Kitchens and return to the airfield in time to meet me and return to the Mess on another bus, doing his best to look as though he was starving.

Always impatient to disembark from the bus, he would sometimes leap out as soon as the folding doors were opened. This was quite an acrobatic feat if the bus had not stopped and it was even funnier when the roadsides were snow banked.

He soon found a girlfriend at a farm quite a distance away and could be a darned nuisance with his amorous ways. Three times in one day I had to retrieve him from the farm, making the journey on a bike. On the last journey back up the hill, I tied him to the handlebars and used his strength to pull me up. That was a good idea until he saw a rabbit in the ditch.

I loved having a dog again and in our time off, usually when it snowed, we would take long walks in the countryside and he would take great leaps into the swollen rivers. We were a great team. He was getting his reward for having had a sedentary life in Manchester and I was having mine after the dirt and dust of North Africa. It was Heaven. The war seemed far away.

I was fortunate again to find a good friend in F/Lt Jackie Burr. He lived in the next room and was very fond of Mac. In consequence he could always be relied upon to take over if I got caught up with night flying or wished to go to the cinema or to a dance. Jackie was tall, dark, handsome and was a Londoner who had spent a lot of his war flying Hurricanes in defence of convoys.

The Hurricanes were carried aboard a merchant ship in a convoy and these ships were known as CAM Ships (Catapult Aircraft Merchantmen). Cordite charges and a catapult system was used to launch the Hurricanes which were only used as defence when the convoys were beyond range of shore-based fighters. The well documented Arctic Convoys to Russia were thus protected. The job was a one-way ticket affair, for after launching, the Hurricane could not be recovered. Ditching or baling out was the only hope of survival.

Survival time in Arctic waters was thought to be fifteen minutes, so arrival into the sea by whatever manner chosen had to be close to a friendly ship which might or might not be prepared to stop if under attack.

Jackie had collected a DFC when with the PQ18 convoy to Russia. He had been launched from MS Empire Morn in September 1942. Having survived that, he was unfortunately killed in a flying accident when instructing at night soon after we left Montrose. Such are the fortunes of war.

I was writing regularly to Betty and no doubt we had an understanding that all things being equal we would probably marry when the war was finished. However, she was a poor communicator and would not happily use the telephone. In this case absence was not to make the heart grow fonder and I found myself flirting about with one or two local girls, but my dog still occupied most of my spare time.

Learning to become a flying instructor was mainly a DIY affair. We were issued with a book with an Air Publication Number and from this we learned 'The Patter'. Every manoeuvre had its patter and this had to be known almost word perfect, similar to learning a part for a play. Of course every pilot had his own ways of explaining and demonstrating, but to a great extent the method was stereotyped. It was this that made RAF pilot training so good. A pupil could switch from one instructor to another without a great deal of disruption. With regular checks from senior instructors and by constantly flying with each other, we progressed.

Jackie Burr and I flew a lot together as pilot or pupil alternately. I was writing to Sherry about once a week and had arranged to see her again in March, but with my own amorous affairs I was not progressing very well. As a young lover I suspect I was an unmitigated disaster, which was not surprising looking back over the past years.

When aged seventeen, despite the uplifting experience of the draughty hole in the wall, I was living in the strict moral confines of a Victorian, God-fearing household. At eighteen, Barclays Bank and the YMCA were hardly the breeding grounds of carnal sin and from then on my life in the Royal Air Force was spent either on the hoof and not staying long enough in an area to overcome the kiss on the doorstep barrier, or being more interested in mastering the art of flying than mastering females.

The mid-Texas affair and resulting uncomfortable balls had awoken something within me, but not a lot, and a one night stand in London was over so quickly I could not recall much of what had transpired. So, here I was at the age of twenty-two, still slightly mystified by women.

Sometimes an opportunity to plumb the depths of the subject would come my way, but I was always to fail on the run in. Invariably, memories of the films shown at Swiss Cottage in the recruiting days would ruin any chance of an involvement.

Even the short time spent at Montrose had served up a moment which had been dashed by my inability to 'rise to the occasion'. The opportunity arose in the closing hours of a Mess dance, when I persuaded a young lady to take a walk through the snow to meet my dog. One thing led to another, but I finally left her warming her toes at the meagre fire in my room.

I returned to the Mess Bar where I met a fellow pilot who was later to become my son's Godfather. I told him of my dilemma and he offered to give the lady my apologies for my extended absence. An hour later he returned, his large fair moustache bristling and with a grin like the cat who had stolen the cream. We did not discuss the eventualities but it was obviously a case of "it is an ill wind that blows nobody any good."

A NEW BEGINNING

The deep winter was over and the lighter evenings of early March gave Scotland an air of charm that I had hitherto not experienced. I liked the Scots people and their open ways, the moors and the never-ending stretches of clean rivers. I took a penchant to Tartan and decided to become eccentric.

I bought many pairs of Tartan socks and wore them always with my uniform despite protests from authority. To many colleagues I was 'The chap with the Springer Spaniel and Tartan socks' and I began to feel mature.

Despite all the happenings of the last three and a half years, despite the anxieties and tragedies, I must admit to having behaved like an overgrown schoolboy. Now, with the Instructors' course coming to a close, I knew I was to have new responsibilities. Soon I would be at a Flying Training School and the overgrown schoolboys would be my pupils. What I was to teach them and the way I did it, could either make or mar their lives.

Similar to people on holiday not making acquaintance until the final day, our course became very chummy, not only amongst ourselves but to other permanent members of the Mess and to the Mess servants.

Because of the dog and my constant journeys to the kitchens for his dinner, I was very well known to the cooks and waitresses. I used to repay their kindness by small gifts in the form of drinks for the men and rationed chocolate for the girls.

I became very friendly with a sweet fair-haired Scottish lassie, 'J', a WAAF waitress who sometimes served in the bar. She hailed from nearby Aberdeen and she spoke with the attractive lilt of those parts. In a mad moment of impetuous confidence I asked her if she would accompany me to Dundee at the weekend.

Further chat on the subject revealed that to shop, dine and dance would take until 11:00 pm, and there were no trains we could catch back to Montrose. I was quite charmed with the lady and was delighted when she said she was prepared to stay overnight. I asked Jackie Burr to look after the dog and a meeting at the station was arranged as 'J' and I thought that we should not be seen leaving the Mess together.

At breakfast on the Saturday 'J' was on duty and we could not resist a warm smile, one to the other. My colleagues being what they were, knew of our impending meeting but treated the matter with the dignity it deserved. All that is with the exception of one moustachioed chauvinist who said fairly loudly that I should have a good weekend because the lady (as he crudely put it) "Banged like a rabbit." There was some laughter and I was glad to leave the table.

The journey to Dundee that afternoon was fun and 'J' looked lovely in her party dress. As the day went by, I realised her looks did not belie her nature. She was as sweet as a spring flower.

The afternoon turned to evening and I booked a double room at an Hotel where we ate before leaving for the Floral Hall. We danced together all the evening and knew we liked each other very much. We danced closer and exchanged kisses in the darker corners of the dance floor. The last waltz was played and we made for our hotel.

We both tensed somewhat as the room door closed behind us. She bathed and I climbed in after her, but we were both very discreet. I entered the room again as she was pulling her nightie over her head. In her soft Scots voice she asked, "Do you mind if I keep my knickers on?"

Being a man of the world I readily agreed that it was a reasonable request from a well-brought-up girl. As we settled into bed, clinging close to each other for warmth, she was shivering like a leaf in a gale and I asked if she was cold. She replied that she was not, but just plain frightened. I re-assured her and buried my face into the collar of her Winceyette nightie and tried to sleep.

During the night we caressed and kissed occasionally and I did enjoy the warmth of her breasts. We were up early and soon back to the Mess at Montrose.

'J' was on duty again and looked at me quite lovingly as she served lunch. I had hardly slept a wink during the night and was feeling a bit touchy and tired. I noticed my chauvinistic moustachioed friend eye 'J's' trim figure as she disappeared into the kitchens.

He got as far as remarking "Bangs like .." when he caught the warning look in my bloodshot eye and stopped short. It was just as well for him as he nearly got the contents of my soup plate over his head.

'J' and I went to some more dances locally before I was to return South. Each occasion was warm and affectionate. We both knew that each had got out of that trip to Dundee exactly what was wanted; no more, no less. As far as women were concerned, I still had a lot to learn.

In that frame of mind I caught the train to my new posting, 17 SFTS.

"Where is Cranwell?" someone asked.

"Dunno" I replied, "somewhere on the East Coast I think."

An explanatory note on the fact that I was not certain of Cranwell's locality lies in that in the pre-war days, the populace did not move about the country anywhere approaching the way it does today. The reason was simple, as not too many people were able to afford motor cars and the resulting ease that the form of travel took with it.

Most people knew where Blackpool, Bournemouth, Brighton, Bridlington and Skegness were, but villages and small towns near any of these places were unheard of if one did not come from the locality.

The Berryman families were privileged to own cars. Nevertheless even by 1944 I had not travelled the country widely and only knew the South and South-West regions. The furthest North I had ever travelled was Nottingham or Great Yarmouth and to Liverpool and Glasgow to board troopships. So despite travelling over a great deal of the USA and North Africa, of my own country I was still only interested in the sectors and airfields I was flying over regularly.

I could have named and found most airfields in the South and West but for anything North of London I would have had to resort to a map. Hence, not knowing the exact whereabouts of Cranwell was understandable under the circumstances.

Proceeding South overnight on the train, I looked up Cranwell and found to my surprise that it was only 15 miles from Lincoln, Sherry and David.

I was very tired when I arrived at Mr and Mrs Parker's home, where Sherry was living and after a meal I took a snooze on the couch in the Drawing Room. I was awakened at four in the afternoon by Sherry and the baby.

We looked at each other and I sleepily smiled. I asked if she would marry me.

"Yes", she replied immediately – and there I was 'Catched'.

I went on to London and informed my parents of my decision and they came to the conclusion that I had taken leave of my senses. A once-widowed woman might have been acceptable, but twice and with a child was a bit much for their Victorian views. Fortunately they had met Ray and Sherry, so they were able to understand my feelings in the matter. It was just that the whole concept of such an enormous step, from boyhood to pilot to married man and father in five war-torn years, when we had seen so little of one another was almost beyond their understanding.

I was due for a few days leave which I took in London and I arrived at Cranwell in the closing days of March to start a tour of duty as a Flying Instructor. However, it was not long before the boss decided that my dog, my tartan socks and I would be better placed beyond the confines of the holy of holy's, Cranwell College.

The satellite airfield to Cranwell was at Wellingore and there was living accommodation there. Working from Wellingore was ideal; Mac enjoyed the freedom of the surrounding woods and we were both in our element again. A cycle ride from the Mess to flights was always enjoyable with Mac bounding along beside me and stopping for his drink of water at a farm stand pipe. I could get to see Sherry and David once or twice during the week and every Sunday.

The trip of twelve miles was made very easy as I could get an allocation of rationed petrol. Valerie (Sherry) was allowed the use of her Father's SS Jaguar 12, a beautiful car to look at and drive. Sometimes I would stay in Lincoln on the Sunday night and would be dropped off on the Monday morning right alongside the aircraft I was to use for the first instructional flight of the day. Before Valerie had reached the main road to Lincoln on the return journey, she would be buzzed by a Harvard still tucking its wheels away.

Life at Wellingore was very relaxed and I was obviously in love, as I sometimes picked primroses from the woods and presented them to Valerie.

David was a noisy child and never seemed to stop crying. If he did he would only stop long enough to pee on me. Perhaps, this was the only way he could protest about the fact that I was shortly to marry his Mother and become his Dad.

Germany was nearly engulfed by Allied troops but still they fought on, always in retreat. Somehow or other it would surely end soon. I felt sad for the troops still slogging it out but was quite content with Wellingore and the new job. I enjoyed instructing and found the work rewarding and challenging with unlimited scope for the beloved aerobatics.

Early April I took Valerie to Ealing where Father and Mother were about to celebrate their Silver Wedding. We all had a great party, made all the more enjoyable by the anticipation of the War ending and victory for the Allies. The only tears at Queen Annes Gardens that night were tears of joy as Valerie was accepted as my wife to be.

May saw a move of 17 STFS to Spitalgate near Grantham. In the same month I stood in the bar celebrating VE Day. It was a sober affair and we felt quite lost. Realisation dawned that we should soon be out of a job unless the Japanese war wanted us. As single-engined pilots, the chances of that were minimal as there were plenty of multi-engined pilots available.

For now however, there was work to be done and the flying was good. Valerie and I were still getting to know one other, and one day she asked me to help her sort some of Ray's personal and RAF belongings. We went through a pile of papers, old flying gloves and such like.

I opened a box containing more papers, beneath which I was amazed to find the Bulova watch which had belonged to one of the two pilots suspended at the time of Jock Craig's death in 1942. It did not pass into Ray's possession at the time and how it got there remains a mystery. Like my Bulova it still works.

Without trauma, Valerie and I accepted that we could never have a beginning to marriage as would normally be expected as there was always the baby to consider. We were very happy when we married at St Giles' Church, Lincoln on May 26th 1945 and family, friends and my fellow instructors were there to see us joined together in Holy Matrimony.

Brother Alan was my Best Man and very nearly missed the service when he became totally engrossed with Lincoln Cathedral and misjudged his timing. He had the ring in his possession and the usual ring removing struggle took place amongst the ladies. Eventually, with a bang and a crash of the church doors he was at my side, smartly dressed in his Army uniform as he had joined the Forces in September 1944. It was fortuitous that he had no words to say, as he had no breath left with which to say them.

Then with the service over we all repaired to the Grand Hotel Lincoln for a small reception, after which Valerie and I poured our guests into taxis and trains for their homes before leaving for our newly-acquired abode, a flat at No. 164 Harrowby Road, Grantham.

We were now using Valerie's car, a Standard 9 similar to that I had used in 1943. It was loaded to the maximum with wedding presents and all the paraphernalia that goes with a ten month old baby as we set off for Grantham in the rain.

It was only an hour's journey, but David cried all the way and upon arrival I found I had forgotten the key to the flat. I was damp and fed up as I broke a downstairs window to admit my new family. I did not carry my bride over the threshold as I hadn't the strength left. David continued to cry most of the night and when I reported to flights the next morning with eyes hanging down like a dog's balls, my colleagues pulled my leg about an amorous night. That was the last straw.

I had three good pupils and the way they were progressing boded well for their ultimate success. At the start of the course I had experienced one hiccup when I was allocated a student who could do nothing right for me.

I considered him dangerous and asked for him to be checked out by a senior instructor. The check out showed no great faults in his airmanship and he was returned to me to proceed with his training. He was a very pleasant young man and he appeared to like me, but nevertheless he still continued to do the most stupid things. I got so used to him attempting to raise the undercarriage instead of the flaps after landing, that I used to jam the control with my feet as soon as the aircraft stopped rolling.

His steep turns were so uncontrolled that the aircraft would judder like a pneumatic drill before he would make a correction. I asked for him to be checked again. He flew well for another instructor, resulting in his removal from my charge and substitution of another pupil.

In retrospect I consider all this trauma was a direct cause of my inexperience as a flying instructor, coupled with the fact that the lad was constantly nervous with me and was trying too hard. With another instructor he did well.

Meanwhile my three pupils passed out high up the course ladder (a very good example of 'Horses for Courses'). For me it was a lesson learned and I realised that I had much to learn about instructing, mostly psychology.

Spitalgate had an influx of other flying units and the circuit became very crowded with air traffic, resulting in No 2 Squadron of 17 STFS flying from Harlaxton nearby.

Valerie and I were well settled in our new home in Grantham and in order to eke out the meagre petrol ration I received for the car, I purchased a motor cycle. This time it was a 1929 model complete with oil and fuel primers and only 7 years younger than I. Riding this machine was an experience I would have been sad to have missed, especially when climbing a hill necessitated considerable paddle action with the legs for extra propulsion.

The joyful days were not to last too long, thanks I think to the powers of the press. The occasion of Valerie's third wedding to a third pilot in three years invoked considerable comment in the popular press and headlines such as "Third Time Lucky" appeared.

I have no way of proving that my removal from flying duties exactly one month after the wedding was the result of intervention by someone in high authority, but I have always suspected it. On the other hand, perhaps it was The Highest Authority who had the last say, and perhaps I should be grateful. After all, I had survived almost four years of war-time flying and rubbed shoulders with some of the finest men I should meet in my lifetime. I had learned more about determination, overwhelming fear, consuming disappointments and love – but not hate, which was something I had not experienced, not even for the enemy who would have blasted me out of the sky given the chance. Above all I had learned to respect myself.

On June 26th, 1945 I flew a last formation with a pupil I had previously never flown with. Breaking from the formation high over Lincoln Cathedral I told him to relax and I would fly. I pointed the nose South towards Grantham and base, began a gentle dive and rolled and rolled and rolled all the way home. I have never had much inclination to fly straight and level since. When the flying stopped, I developed a rather discomforting period of nervous reaction and was unable to concentrate very long at anything. I became extremely impatient and intolerant, particularly with regard to rules and regulations. I had a feeling that nothing mattered any more. Given a heap of leave passes to sign in order to relieve the station adjutant, I distinctly remember signing every one either as 'Julius Caesar' or 'Henry the Eighth'. I was not bothered, neither it seemed was anyone else. Then the Atom bombs were dropped and Japan surrendered.

The war was over.

There was great rejoicing throughout the land and the RAF fortuitously relieved my nervous tension by making me feel important again. I was to take a three month Physical Fitness Officers' Course at Cosford near Wolverhampton. I would be able to help in keeping fit and relieving the boredom of the thousands of men and women waiting to return to civilian life. It was the first course ever and suited me well with my natural aptitude for games, callisthenics and athletics. I enjoyed Cosford and so did Mac. I got home to see Valerie and David very little in those three months and they were now living with her parents.

At the conclusion of the course I found myself as PFO to RAF Peterborough until it closed when I found myself embarrassed as an inventory holder to find that the NAAFI clock had been misappropriated. No doubt it still ticks merrily away in an ageing gentleman's home somewhere.

While at Peterborough on December 13th, 1945 Valerie presented me with the son I very much wanted. Nicholas Wyndham and David Raymund each had a half brother. With Peterborough closed I moved to Kirton Lindsay near Lincoln and continued as a PFO.

Time was beginning to drag as more and more personnel were demobbed. On occasions I got away to help Mr Parker, my Father-in-Law, in his motor business where I learned that cars were in short supply and in demand. My entrepreneurial heritage showed itself and I began buying and selling motor cars to augment my income which had now risen to exactly £30 a month.

Mr Parker became ill and I obtained compassionate leave to look after his business for him. Not knowing the intimate details of a car's workings, this was not easy. Somehow I got by long enough for him to recover. On his return to business he suggested that I should join him in running the garage. This was somewhat disturbing as I was quite resolved to return to the Bank. His offer of £5 a week with a few perks was too much to resist and I retired from the RAF to join him on the last day of July 1946.

I knew that the past five years were probably to be the most exciting in my life, but there was a great opportunity ahead and I wanted to rise to the challenge.

Sometimes, when working with a grease gun in one hand and a broom in the other, I would hear the sigh of a Merlin engine overhead and Mac and I would rush outside to catch a glimpse of a Hurricane or a Spitfire.

My heart would nearly stop with excitement and I would feel empty and sick of stomach as it disappeared. I did yearn to relive some of those wonderful moments when I had taken the wings of a bird to swoop and soar above the earth.

Photos

Grandmother, Minnie.

Grandfather, William.

Grandmother, Emily.

My parents in 1939.

No 10 Queen Anne's Gardens – our family home throughout the war.

Father and his Humber

My two boys, David McNair Taylor and Nicholas Berryman with McNT 1948.

Self and brother Alan.

*Family members 'doing their bit: (above)
Alan (sgt, Father (Captain) and myself (Erk).
(left) Cousin Ken, Sergeant Armourer.*

*Myself and
cousin Ken, 40
years on.*

Muriel England – 'Cis' – photographed in Torquay in 1941. We loved very innocently, but she went out of my life tragically six months later when she died of Tuberculosis. The back of the photo reads:

"To Nick, with best wishes, Cis."

A more intimate message was written in Morse code:

"I love you now, I will love you always."

Clair Compton lived with her wealthy parents in the nicest area of Dallas. Her father was a Dallas advocate and an ardent prohibitionist but Clair could drink most of us under the table.

She and I developed a pleasant friendship. We danced, swam and partied. I hardly needed money, as she always paid if I couldn't, and her car was at my disposal at weekends.

PT 17s at Arcadia, Florida USA.

Terrell Texas

(above from left to right:) myself, Cooke, Rees, Humphrey, Campbell.

(left, top) Jock Craig, a young Scot from Dundee who was killed when he crashed in flames after hitting a radio beacon mast while low flying.

(left, bottom) the wreckage of Jock's aircraft.

The click of the shutter whilst taking this photograph caused Ian Campbell's horse to bolt...

Two hours later he returned with his uniform trousers in ribbons...

Courageously, Ian smiled through it all.

But sadly, he was to die in Italy 16 months later.

Having survived baling out of his 111 Squadron Spitfire, he was shot dead whilst attempting to escape.

A 'shagbat' gets a little help from the Royal Navy.

(left to right) myself, Elder, McSween, Feeney, McKay, Frisby, Hannah.

Jeanie, batwoman supreme.

'Gibby' – a brave Walrus navigator.

Invaluable ground crew at Warmwell.

(left to right) Bird, Elder, Renvoize, Hanna, Scott, Kirkby, Feeney..

Some of No.7 Course, Terrell Texas.

My good friend Paul Mercer, who was killed flying a Whirlwind against the Munsterland on 24th October 1943.

Visiting Father in the Home Guard.

Celebrating a rescue, Warmwell 1943 –
(left to right): Scott & Galloway, Porter, Bird, self, Kirkby.

'Jas' Storrar in the 1940s.

Ronald Fairfax Hamlyn.

Harold Arthur Cooper Bird-Wilson.

Dennis 'Hurricane' David.

Ray McNair Taylor.

Paul Mercer.

The Walrus, affectionately known as the 'shagbat'. If I had to choose, I would say that the Walrus was the most exciting of all the aircraft I flew.

Spitfire AQ-D on its nose. One of my less successful take-offs!

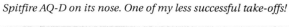

Derna Harbour, North Africa, May 13th 1944.

Taking a bath in the desert.

*Author with PT 17
Arcadia, Florida USA.*

Myself and McNT, always together.

McNT at Wellingore.

Valerie's first wedding to Roger Bokobza, 14th November, 1942.

Valerie's second wedding to Ray McNair-Taylor, 24th August 1943.